T0345020

"The book goes a long way toward raising the profile of the invaluable role enterprise architects play in major software initiatives. For this reason, I have confidence that if organizations take these insights to heart and leverage them effectively, they will begin to deliver consistent, real returns on their IT investments. Will this book make a difference? Time will tell, but my sense is that it very well can."

—William M. Ulrich, President at Tactical Strategy Group, Inc.

Confessions of an Enterprise Architect

Confessions of an Enterprise Architect is the insider's track on how to succeed as an enterprise architect despite the politics, budgets, setbacks, personnel issues, and technological challenges. It includes theoretical and pragmatic discussions about the discipline, imparts constructive recommendations born of personal experience, and presents a set of best practices for developing professional-caliber architectures that deliver professional-caliber systems.

The book also features numerous "Confessions," which are practical tips, warnings, and guidance from a practicing enterprise architect garnered over a career of independent practice. A sample of confessions includes:

- Accommodating change is the sole constant in the professional life of an enterprise architect
- Many enterprise architects don't appreciate that their decisions not only affect system design but also impact the development environment and influence the structure of project teams
- In many cases, initial project estimates are so inaccurate that approvers would be better off developing their own assessments
- In many project teams, the user is the last consideration

The insights contained in this book, typified by its "Confessions" and "Pro Tips," offer organizations a way forward with enterprise architecture. This book also explains how enterprise architects can engage senior business leaders as effectively and as fluently as engaging business analysts, developers, business professionals, program managers, and fellow architects. In addition, it demonstrates how to communicate sophisticated, leading-edge concepts in clean, simple ways that facilitate buy-in at every level. Most importantly, the book makes the case that a professional enterprise architect—and, by extension, a professional-caliber enterprise architecture—sets the foundation for continued success in an industry accustomed to failure.

Confessions of an Enterprise Architect

By
Charles F. Bowman

CRC Press
Taylor & Francis Group
Boca Raton London New York

CRC Press is an imprint of the
Taylor & Francis Group, an **informa** business

AN AUERBACH BOOK

First edition published 2024
by CRC Press
2385 Executive Center Drive, Suite 320, Boca Raton FL 33431

and by CRC Press
4 Park Square, Milton Park, Abingdon, Oxon, OX14 4RN

CRC Press is an imprint of Taylor & Francis Group, LLC

© 2024 Plenum Press, LLC

ISBN: 978-1-032-51718-6 (hbk)
ISBN: 978-1-032-12077-5 (pbk)
ISBN: 978-1-003-41428-5 (ebk)

DOI: 10.1201/9781003414285

Typeset in Cobol
by Deanta Global Publishing Services, Chennai, India

*This book is dedicated to every individual willing
to confront the dragons of fear.
Please be assured, you are not alone.*

Contents

Foreword xi
Preface xv
Acknowledgments xvii
Author xix

Chapter 1 Incite to Insight 1

Chapter 2 What Is Enterprise Architecture? 9

Chapter 3 The Role of an Enterprise Architect 47

Chapter 4 Decisions, Decisions, Decisions 81

Chapter 5 Essential Design Principles 101

Chapter 6 Building Large-Scale Systems 121

Chapter 7 The Life and Times of an Enterprise Architect 157

Chapter 8 What Causes Projects to Fail? 189

Chapter 9 What Is the Future Role of the Enterprise Architect?..... 233

Appendix.. 241

Index 265

Contents

Chapter 1

Chapter 2

Chapter 3

Chapter 4

Chapter 5

Chapter 6

Chapter 7

Chapter 8

Foreword

When I was asked to write this foreword for *Confessions of an Enterprise Architect*, I was unsure what to expect. I have worked with many organizations on multiple initiatives where enterprise architects were involved at one level or another. The role, while varying from organization to organization, always seemed to lack what it takes to gain respect from senior business leaders. In fact, as I am writing this foreword, I had a call with a client who told me that her executives just disbanded the company's enterprise architecture team for many of the reasons cited in this book. I have heard this same story from a number of organizations over the years. The ongoing abandonment of enterprise architecture teams is one clear sign that the many foibles associated with enterprise architects, so clearly articulated in this book, are not a historic curiosity item but a very real and immediate concern for organizations today.

I must make a couple of my own confessions. The first is that having a wealth of experience working with enterprise architects, I entered the task of drafting this foreword with certain opinions on their role in organizations. Frankly, I was never entirely clear as far as what role enterprise architects are supposed to play. Most of my experience with enterprise architects found them to be too into the technical weeds, having little or no understanding of business, data, or application architectures. I also found enterprise architects to varying degrees detached from reality where, in a few cases, I am pretty sure a few of the individuals I worked with never actually met someone in the business community or had an interest in doing so. In my experience, many enterprise architects are so consumed with drawing models and exploring the latest technologies that addressing real business issues was the furthest thing from their minds. To echo several business leaders I have worked with, enterprise architects are stuck in an ivory tower, drain enterprise budgets, and contribute little in terms of business value.

My second confession is that author Charlie Bowman and I worked together on a multiyear initiative representing a portfolio investment of well over $100 million at a very old institution with highly entrenched thinking. My role was strategic business architect, and Charlie's was chief architect.

We broke new ground on that effort, leveraging architecture to link business strategy through solution deployment. A true polymath, Charlie engaged senior business leaders as easily and as fluently as he engaged business analysts, developers, business professionals, program managers, and fellow architects, communicating sophisticated, leading-edge concepts in clean, simple ways, and gaining buy-in at every level. In my view, the author of this book walks the walk, which is why I agreed to write this foreword and why people should read this book.

There is some good news, however; the book delivers much more than a list of grievances against enterprise architects; it offers a justification, coupled with a viable path forward, for organizations to correct the situation. It makes the case that a viable enterprise architect function is essential because the role it should be playing in initiative execution remains largely unfilled, which in turn undermines successful initiative deployment and the ability to achieve the strategies those initiatives seek to deliver. In other words, disbanding the enterprise architecture team and scattering enterprise architects to the four winds is not the solution and will only make a bad situation worse. Allow me to highlight one of the more glaring cases in point.

An important subtext that runs through much of the book is that when push comes to shove, business leaders are quick to jettison architecture, impact analysis, requirements, and testing, much to the detriment of the solutions they are seeking. This reflexive tendency is the norm, not the exception, and the rigor this book promotes seeks to reverse this thinking. Consider this simple yet profound statement in Chapter 8 that caught my attention:

> When a business leader starts a sentence with "Wouldn't it be great if we could ..." there is a high likelihood that this statement will launch an initiative with no clear scope, cost-benefit analysis, or target state.

In my experience, these or similar words have launched countless initiatives, the vast majority of which fell short of their objective or failed entirely. Not so coincidentally, initiative estimates and corresponding budgets are off the mark by a factor of two or more. The cause in large part has to do with jumping from impulse to execution, which, as Charlie puts it, is unique to the world of software development. The enterprise architect is not alone in stopping these knee-jerk investments, but a strong enterprise architect can go a long way toward keeping these situations from going over a proverbial cliff.

As far as highlighting the long list of factors that have poisoned the minds of many management teams on the role of the enterprise architect, this book does not sugarcoat the situation. It is packed with truths about the role of enterprise architect. In fact, when one reads the thoughtful, well-researched list of issues that have dogged enterprise architecture teams and enterprise architects for so many years, one gets the idea that the situation is just too far gone to be corrected. I have always felt that reversing the current thinking on the value of the enterprise architect was beyond anyone's reach. Yet this book goes a long way toward doing just that. Page after page, chapter after chapter, I was struck by the real-world issues raised and the insightful guidance addressing those issues. It is my firm opinion that if business leaders read and act upon the lessons in this book, there is a real chance that the role of the enterprise architect can gradually be redeemed but, more importantly, enterprise architecture as a profession can begin to fill critical architecture gaps on initiatives large and small.

If it is not clear to this point, I want to emphasize that the insights and guidance Charlie lays out so clearly in this book are not based on conjecture but on real-world experience gained through multiple, large-scale initiatives across multiple industries. This book provides readers and organizations with valuable insights regardless of whether you have an enterprise architecture team, abandoned your enterprise architecture team, or never had an enterprise architecture team in the first place. Readers are well advised to not just read it, but share it with peers and business leaders. The book goes a long way toward raising the profile of the invaluable role enterprise architects play in major software initiatives. For this reason, I have confidence that if organizations take these insights to heart and leverage them effectively, they will begin to deliver consistent, real returns on their IT investments. Will this book make a difference? Time will tell, but my sense is that it very well can.

William M. Ulrich
September 2022

Preface

Including the word "Confessions" in the title of this book is deliberately evocative. However, my motives for doing so were pure.

Really.

My sole objective is to entice you to join me in taking a peek behind the curtain to see what transpires in the labyrinthian and cavernous confines of IT organizations.

You see, over the decades, some software shops have acquired reputations ranging from bungling to bewildering. Sadly, in many cases, such characterizations are well deserved.

Consequently, stakeholders—spanning the gamut from perplexed senior executives to baffled end users—have tried to discover the best ways to "feed the beast" and impel development shops to deliver applications that meet their needs. But unfortunately, this has proved challenging to achieve, let alone replicate.

However, despite popular preconceptions, the problems are not unilateral. On the contrary, as I reveal throughout this book, there are many causes and culprits that contribute to the ever-growing pile of failed development projects. Nevertheless, because they deliver the final product, IT shops often find themselves standing alone, centered squarely in the crosshairs of criticism.

I guess you could argue that's the nature of the job. And to some extent, you'd be right.

Nevertheless, I think it's high time all stakeholders assume their share of accountability and acknowledge that, like the computer systems they develop, IT shops are also subject to the GIGO principle—Garbage In, Garbage Out. Inadequate requirements, ineffectual project management, and conflicting objectives can all—and commonly do—contribute to a project's demise. I'm so tired of watching the efforts—often extraordinary sacrifices—of many committed team members get squandered because of the ignorance, incompetence, inexperience, indifference, and intransigence of a few inexpert individuals. And who hasn't grown weary of checkbook-brandishing stakeholders who, because they wield the power to *decide*, believe that makes them unerringly *right*?

So, this raises the question: As an Enterprise Architect, how do you navigate the roiling, storm-tossed oceans of system development, which are subject to the ever-changing tides of the marketplace, the churning undercurrents of organizational politics, the swirling eddies of uncertainty, and the turbulent maelstroms of poor leadership?

Carefully and cautiously.

But that answer is way too terse and way too trite, which is why I authored this book. I want to expose the underlying mismanagement, misconduct—and, dare I say, malpractice—undermining many development projects. In addition, I'd like to share some advice and key learnings I've garnered over the 40-some-odd years I've spent sailing these murky waters that will help keep you afloat in even the most tumultuous seas.

It might not be *The Old Man and the Sea*, but someone must tell this fish tale. So, hop aboard, matey. We're about to weigh anchor and make some waves.

Acknowledgments

Although only one name appears on the cover of this book, a project of this size requires the contributions of many dedicated professionals. I am grateful to all of them.

I want to begin by thanking my Editor, John Wyzalek, for his patience and suggestions that made the authoring of this book as pleasant as possible.

During development, a manuscript undergoes many critiques. The suggestions of the following reviewers made this book a better read:

- My friend and business partner, Joseph Cerasani
- My friend and colleague, William M. Ulrich

That said, any errors or omissions are mine alone.

I'd also like to thank the excellent staff at CRC Press, who shepherded the manuscript through all the production phases. Their dedicated professionalism is evident in the quality of the book.

Finally, I'd like to thank my family for their enduring support and Maria for always being there when I need her.

Author

Charles F. Bowman is a managing partner of Polygon Partners, LLC, a consulting and training firm specializing in emerging technologies. As an independent consultant, Mr. Bowman has over 40 years of experience developing large-scale software systems and has served as Enterprise Architect for numerous clients.

Mr. Bowman is a popular speaker who has lectured throughout the United States, Canada, the United Kingdom, Australia, Switzerland, and Germany. In addition, as an adjunct lecturer for St. John's University and City University of New York, he has taught undergraduate and graduate classes in a wide range of subjects, including *Algorithms & Data Structures*, *Database Design*, and *Compiler Construction*.

Mr. Bowman has been a regular columnist for *The X Journal, Client/Server Developer, The Java Report*, and *Distributed Object Computing*. In addition, he has served as editor-in-chief for several journals, including *The X Journal, UNIX Developer*, and *CORBA Development,* and as series editor for the *Managing Object Technologies* book series of Cambridge University/SIGs Books and the *How Things Work Series* by CRC Press.

Mr. Bowman's other books include *Algorithms and Data Structures: An Approach in C* (Harcourt Brace, 1994); *Objectifying Motif* (SIGs Books, 1995); *Wisdom of the Gurus* (SIGs Books, 1996); *Broadway: the Complete Internet Architecture* (Addison Wesley Longman, 2000); *How Things Work: The Computer Science Edition* (CRC Press, 2022); and *How Things Work: The Technology Edition* (CRC Press, 2023).

A graduate of New York's prestigious Brooklyn Technical High School, Mr. Bowman holds a BS in Computer Science from St. John's University and an MS in Computer Science from New York University.

1

Incite to Insight

If you want to truly understand something, try to change it.

—Kurt Lewin

Change is the only constant. Hanging on is the only sin.

—Denise McCluggage

INTRODUCTION

This is my rant—but I'm already getting ahead of myself.

I've spent the better part of a professional lifetime—over 40 years—working in IT. And as it turned out, my career has tracked in lockstep the computer industry's emergence, expansion, and ultimate ascendancy. So, I can genuinely say that I've been there every step of the way.

During my career, I've worked on monolithic systems, distributed systems, time-sharing systems, real-time systems, single-user systems, multiuser systems, and cloud-based systems. I've held titles such as junior programmer, senior programmer, system test engineer, application developer, user interface designer, team lead, project lead, application architect, solutions architect, data architect, chief architect, and Enterprise Architect (EA).

DOI: 10.1201/9781003414285-1

I've designed and developed software for operating systems and applications, backends and frontends, controllers, and Database Management Systems (DBMSs). I've had the privilege of contributing to some genuinely innovative and leading-edge systems and experienced the displeasure of watching many others go the way of the dinosaur, the dodo bird, and the Commodore Pet.

I was an employee of one of the largest companies in the world and some of the smallest. I've also been an independent contractor, managing a consulting practice for over 30 years.

But don't worry. I'm not about to bore you with anecdotes of glorious successes or impose melancholy lamentings over the demise of [insert the name of your favorite fossilized technology here]. No, that type of rant is for another book and would require a generous measure of an adult libation.

On the contrary, I intend to focus on what I believe is a much more significant aspect of anyone's career: experience. That is, despite the leapfrogging advances in computer-related technologies, the lessons and skills I've acquired remain surprisingly relevant—particularly as an Enterprise Architect.

My objective is to share those with you.

That last comment, however, brings me to my first point: This book is not another treatise on Enterprise Architecture, espousing the next be-all-end-all design methodology that is so simple it requires only one developer (part-time, of course!), two business analysts (if they're not too busy), three cloud-based computers (who buys hardware anymore?), and four Post-it notes (after all, documentation is essential). And, naturally, suggesting that you hire yours truly as the erudite, urbane, enterprise-architect-about-town who'll solve all your problems *well* before the first martini—I mean, lunch. Many existing tomes make that claim. The IT world doesn't need another.

Instead, this book is about the *role* of the Enterprise Architect (EA) in modern systems development. It's a practical and realistic look at the qualifications, duties, and expectations required of the individuals who have the power to raise an organization's IT infrastructure design to ever higher engineering plateaus or relegate it to a valley of technological chaos.

In short: This book is *not* about developing great Enterprise *Architecture*. Rather, it's about developing great Enterprise *Architects*.

WHY WRITE THIS BOOK?

One evening, while I was still on the fence about writing this book, my girlfriend and I were at dinner when she recounted a telephone conversation she had with an old friend earlier that day. She said it was great to catch up and reminisce, but the conversation left her slightly confused.

I asked her what she meant.

She said that when her friend asked her what I did for a living, she didn't know what to say.

I pondered my response for a moment. Of course, the most obvious answer was "Enterprise Architect." But my girlfriend knew that already. So, obviously, she needed a more intuitive understanding of my profession.

However, therein lies the rub: How do you describe to a layperson what an Enterprise Architect does?

After some additional thought—and several sips of wine—I finally mumbled something about designing large-scale software systems and quickly changed the subject.

You might wonder why I began a book geared toward IT professionals by relating the foregoing vignette. The reason is that laypeople are not alone in their bewilderment about the role of Enterprise Architects. Indeed, much of the software industry is also awash in confusion.

That is not to say that there aren't myriad definitions. On the contrary, there seem to be as many opinions as there are people.

In the end, my girlfriend's confusion clinched it. So I decided to write a book that hopefully clarifies some of the confusion.

WHAT'S INSIDE THIS BOOK?

As noted above, my intention for authoring this book is to illuminate and explore the role and responsibilities of the professional Enterprise Architect. As such, it contains many examples and "Confessions" of how things work in the real world, as opposed to the Pollyanna-like descriptions depicted in the various textbooks and whitepapers on the subject.

Nonetheless, I don't want to be viewed as an apologist for Enterprise Architects, pointing accusing fingers at all other stakeholders. So, rest assured, I will also underscore how architectural blunders can wreak havoc on an organization and its infrastructure.

To make my points, I will share and discuss many examples drawn from personal experience. (Every scar has a story.) I will also offer suggestions and some "Pro Tips" to avoid or mitigate the highlighted issues.

However, as I am not in the habit of embarrassing anyone (especially myself!), I will ensure that every scenario is so "sanitized" that even the original participants won't recognize them. In other words, *the names have been changed to protect the innocent.*

As you might expect, much of the material presented herein is my opinion, filtered through the lens of my personal experiences. What can I say? That's innate to the human condition. Nonetheless, I hope readers find that I've presented the subject matter as objectively as possible. My goal is to inform and provoke thought, not to proselytize or browbeat anyone with holier-than-thou rhetoric.

As I hope to appeal to a broad audience (see below), I will not assume readers are familiar with the technical aspects of any specific products, architectural models, or methodologies. Thus, when the discussion warrants it, I will describe technical complexities in sufficient detail to avoid confusion. Similarly, I will also provide definitions whenever I introduce jargon. Moreover, the Glossary appearing near the end of the book contains explanations for all the acronyms and terms of art used throughout the text.

One caveat: I've written the chapters so you may read them independently in any sequence. Consequently, I had to repeat some *Confessions* and *Pro Tips* to ensure sections read cohesively.

WHO SHOULD READ THIS BOOK?

Although I cannot overstate their importance in delivering successful IT solutions, Enterprise Architects don't work in a vacuum. In any significant development effort, numerous participants serve in many distinct roles— not all of which are technical. Nonetheless, whether they're aware of it or not, they all contribute to the project's outcome.

Thus, the focus of this book encompasses the entire IT community and should benefit everyone involved in standing up software systems: CIOs,

CTOs, portfolio managers, project managers, team leads, test engineers, business architects, data architects, GUI designers, application developers, etc.

In addition, many "Confessions" and "Pro Tips" will be of particular interest to stakeholders whose organizations are growing through mergers and acquisitions. Establishing and navigating a smooth course through the choppy waters of legacy system integration and consolidation is an extremely unique and special treat.

STAKEHOLDERS, CHARLATANS, AND ARCHITECTS, OH MY!

Regardless of their role, anyone who has participated in designing, developing, and deploying large-scale systems knows firsthand that it's not easy. If it were, there'd be no need for the vast array of books on the subject—including this one.

Unfortunately, however, I believe that, for a wide range of reasons that I will share with you, participants make it harder than necessary. To state it bluntly: It's challenging enough to get all contributors to row in the same direction; what compounds the problem is that they're often on different boats.

Enter the Enterprise Architect.

As we will see, Enterprise Architects wear many hats. But, most importantly, they serve as the focal point for all stakeholders: the "business," the users, project managers, developers, testers, administrators, etc. So, in addition to their "required duties," EAs address gripes, evaluate ideas, resolve disputes, mitigate scheduling conflicts, correct design flaws—well, you get the point. In my experience, successful Enterprise Architects require such diverse skills that they've become modern-day renaissance persons.

But, of course, my view might be slightly biased.

Throughout the remainder of this book, we'll discuss and define the responsibilities and importance of Enterprise Architects in great detail. I will demonstrate the critical role EAs play on the IT stage and how productions can fail or flourish as a result of their direction (or lack thereof).

First, however, I need to digress for a moment and expose the charlatans who undermine the very foundation of this profession.

I did mention that this is a rant, right?

Let the Confessions begin.

Confession 1:

> Anyone can call themselves an Architect.

There may be some readers who might gasp at such a revelation. But regrettably, Confession 1 is all too true.

Sadly, there are no formal qualifications required to assume the title of Architect in the IT world. Thus, anyone can "hang up a shingle"—and, in my experience, many unqualified individuals do just that. Indeed, in many organizations, it's often difficult to swing a dead cat without hitting someone with the title of architect.

Confession 2:

> Anyone can call themselves an Enterprise Architect.

Like their Architect counterparts, there's no need for Enterprise Architects to burden themselves with such mundane impediments as formal education, accredited apprenticeships, or practical experience. Instead, a would-be Enterprise Architect needs only a bit of temerity, enough familiarity with technical jargon to confuse clients, and about $15.00 worth of business cards from Vistaprint.

Let me share an example. I (briefly) worked with one individual who thought that having helped a relative stand up a website afforded him enough experience to design an integrated suite of applications for a trusting—albeit naive—client. The resulting dumpster fire was indeed something to behold.

As you might expect, stakeholders become very wary and extraordinarily skeptical once bitten by a charlatan masquerading as an Enterprise Architect. Indeed, woe on to the next EA they hire.

Unfortunately, even the best EAs can unwittingly compound the problem of distrust simply because they're human.

Confession 3:

Even the best Enterprise Architects are NOT always right.

Shocking, I know.

However, we all make mistakes—even dedicated, talented, professional Enterprise Architects. Unfortunately, this only heightens jaded stakeholders' "buyer beware" mentality when dealing with EAs.

Throughout the remainder of this book, we will address how we can distinguish the professionals from the pretenders.

SUMMARY

In authoring this book, I don't intend to trash systems, methodologies, organizations, or individuals (aside from charlatans masquerading as technologists). Nor do I want to appear arrogantly authoritative, reveling in the failures of others. Such an approach benefits no one and would bore everyone.

I also don't possess the hubris to imagine that I—or this book—will radically alter the world of IT. Sweeping change of that sort requires broad consensus: *It takes a village.*

Nonetheless, I hope that a frank airing of the frustrations, failures, and foibles associated with modern system development will incite thoughtful reflection that will engender meaningful insight. So that if enough folks can recognize and relate to the issues presented herein, maybe, just maybe, some positive change will eventually ensue. And possibly a few Enterprise Architects, once forewarned, will be forearmed for the battles that await them.

We'll see.

Anyway, it's getting late, and I must be getting on with my rant.

2

What Is Enterprise Architecture?

The goal of enterprise architecture is boundary-less information flow, where all systems, IT and non-IT, interoperate.

—Allen Brown

Architecture enables you to accommodate complexity and change. If you don't have Enterprise Architecture, your enterprise is not going to be viable in an increasingly complex and changing external environment.

—John Zachman

INTRODUCTION

I know I promised you a rant—let me assure you, I will fulfill that commitment.

However, before I get on a roll, we must establish some common ground to ensure my ravings have context. After all, I assert that I'm an Enterprise Architect (EA). Thus, I would be remiss if I didn't pour a sound foundation that could support all the stories I intend to layer on it.

So, let's begin with a slight detour that will present a general overview of IT architecture. We will then return to the main road to discuss Enterprise Architecture.

For readers familiar with this material, feel free to skip this chapter. However, you do so at your own risk because I've sprinkled in a few juicy confessions you might regret missing.

DOI: 10.1201/9781003414285-2

WHAT IS IT ARCHITECTURE?

According to many dictionaries, we can define "architecture" as follows:

Definition 1:

> Architecture is the art, science, and practice that focuses on the design and construction of buildings.

In Computer Science, we can define "IT Architecture" as follows:

Definition 2:

> IT Architecture is a formal set of principles, guidelines, and models that informs and directs the design, development, and integration of computer-related components and resources.

Formal IT architectures serve as a blueprint for large-scale application development. They capture and memorialize designs and guide the construction and deployment of computer systems.

Types of Architectures

Developing large-scale automated solutions is far from a trivial undertaking. It requires the coordinated integration of specialized technologies spanning many distinct areas of expertise.

To manage this complexity, the IT industry decomposes the requisite skillsets into distinct (though often overlapping) architectural practices. The following section presents the most common disciplines.

Hardware Architecture	Hardware architecture refers to designing and implementing physical components such as computers, routers, switches, and storage arrays.
Business Architecture	Business Architecture centers on the structure and organization of the enterprise. It

	focuses on an organization's capabilities and strategic objectives.
Systems Architecture	This term refers to designing a suite of components that collectively automate some aspect of an organization's functionality.
Application Architecture	Application Architecture focuses on the design of user-centric systems.
Data Architecture	Data Architecture defines the models, structures, and access strategies for any organization's most valuable non-human resource: data.
Security Architecture	As its name implies, Security Architecture serves as the model through which an organization protects—and provides access to—its electronic resources (both systems and data).
Solutions Architecture	This is a collective term encompassing the implementation architectures (e.g., Application, Data, and Security).

As we will soon see, the preceding collectively forms an Enterprise Architecture.

Common IT Architectural Models

From an abstract perspective, we can decompose most applications into three main sections.

View	This is the part of the application through which users interact with the system. It can be as simple as the display on a digital watch or as complex as the heads-up avionics deployed in modern fighter jets. And the view can change. For example, systems can depict the same data set as a pie chart or a histogram (or both) based on user needs.
Controller	The Controller delivers information to the View and safeguards the integrity of the

data model (see below). Some of its responsibilities include ensuring:

- Users have permission to view or update a given data set.
- Transactions don't violate business rules.
- The integrity of the data model is not compromised.

Data   Data is the most critical aspect of any application, not to mention the most valuable non-human resource of most organizations. Therefore, the system must protect it from both inadvertent and deliberate corruption. Moreover, its design should allow the organization to exploit its full potential.

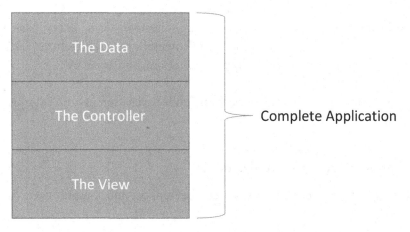

FIGURE 2.1
The Section of an Application

There are many ways to combine and arrange these sections to construct different architectural models. Following are a few descriptions of some of the most common models (Figure 2.1).

However, as you read through this material, please keep in mind that each design approach has a unique set of advantages and disadvantages. Thus, one is not distinctly better than the other; they are just different. Consequently, architects should choose the solution that best fits the project's current and projected future needs.

But before we begin, let me digress for a moment and share a few confessions.

Confession 1:

> Many Enterprise Architects don't address their organization's long-term needs when designing solutions.

Unfortunately, Enterprise Architects often opt for "quick and dirty" designs because they know they will be long gone before the short-sighted approach they've proposed starts fraying at the seams and has become someone else's problem.

Confession 2:

> Like many Enterprise Architects, some stakeholders don't want to address their organization's long-term IT needs.

Sadly, I've found that for some stakeholders, their only goal is to get the problem (i.e., the development of some application) off their plates as quickly as possible. Thus, they adopt the short-sighted position that they'll worry about the future tomorrow. Unfortunately, getting stakeholders with that mindset to appreciate the Return on Investment (ROI) of a sound, robust, and extensible architecture is often too daunting. Indeed, even well-intentioned Enterprise Architects will capitulate when working with such individuals because they don't want to engage in a protracted fight.

To compound the problem, many organizations base project managers' bonus structures on the *number* of applications they deploy rather than the *quality* and *durability* of the systems they develop. Consequently, this practice engenders slapdash rollouts that often lack basic integration features, exhibit poor reliability, and are costly to maintain and extend.

Pro Tip 1:

> As a rule, you should design *holistically* and develop *incrementally*.

Restrictive budgets should constrain resources, not thinking. Always design for the long haul; it's cheaper in the long run.

The following confession will serve as a recurring theme throughout this book.

Confession 3:

You never have enough time for shortcuts.

Unfortunately, short-sightedness is far more prevalent—and much more costly—than you might believe. For example, I've helped clients design their *Next* Next-Generation System before they completed the rollout of their *Current* Next-Generation System. The money, time, and resources squandered in such cases can stagger the mind.

Before I end this digression, I need to state something for the record: The foregoing is NOT a sweeping indictment of ALL rapid development projects. On the contrary, in many cases, a "quick and dirty" strategy is the approach of choice. For example, if you're standing up a system to support a short-lived business initiative, you should spend as little time, money, and resources as possible to accomplish the task.

Okay, enough railing for the moment. Let's return to the main topic: Types of architectures.

Monolithic

As depicted in Figure 2.2, all application sections reside on a single server when employing a monolithic architecture. Due to the prevalence of mainframe computers, monolithic designs were quite common during the early days of IT. All system components ran on a single computer, and users interacted with the system via CRT monitors.[1]

---

1 CRTs (or cathode-ray tubes) were early display devices.

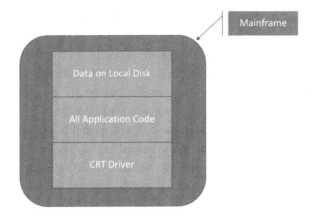

FIGURE 2.2
Monolithic Architecture

For the most part, this model has gone the way of the dinosaur for any reasonably large application because it's slow, complicates development, doesn't scale easily, and the sole server serves as a single point of failure.

However, you may still find monolithic designs occasionally employed in small intelligent devices like smart thermostats.

Client–Server

One of the first approaches to distributed processing, the Client–Server (C/S) architecture allocates functionality across multiple systems. As depicted in Figure 2.3, the View typically acts as the client and resides on an intelligent device (PC, laptop, smartphone, etc.). The remainder of the application resides on the server.

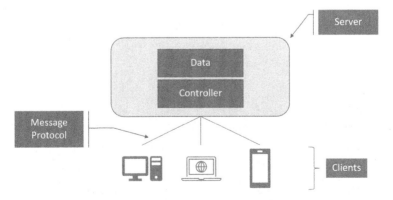

FIGURE 2.3
Example Client–Server Architecture

As its name implies, this model establishes roles: *clients* and *servers*. Clients (e.g., Views) may use and display data as appropriate; servers process transactions and provide data irrespective of the View's design.

This model enables developers to modify clients and servers independently if the inter-component message protocol remains unchanged. Moreover, modern networking facilities allow system designers to distribute and deploy C/S components anywhere on the globe (costs, performance, and permissioning issues aside).

Most modern web-based applications are prime examples of the C/S model. The browser is the view, and the web server is, well, the server.

N-Tier

An N-Tier architecture—also called a Multi-tier architecture—extends the Client–Server model and divides applications into multiple *layers*.[2] The most common is a three-tiered[3] design. See Figure 2.4 for an example.

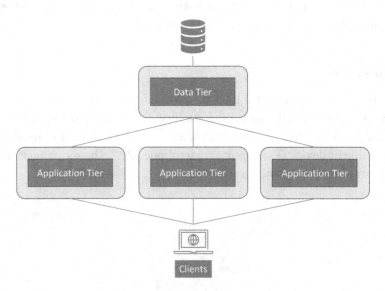

FIGURE 2.4
Three-Tier Architecture

---

2 Technically, the Client–Server model is an N-Tier architecture where *n* equals 2.
3 A Three-Tier model is a variant of the Model–View–Controller Architecture.

Each tier contains one of the application's sections, which runs on independent servers. Although the C/S model relies heavily on network performance, it provides many advantages, including component independence, improved overall performance, and facilitating shared functionality across multiple applications.

As depicted in Figure 2.5, the C/S model allows us to replicate controllers. This design increases overall availability because the system can still provide services to its clients despite a middle-tier component failure.

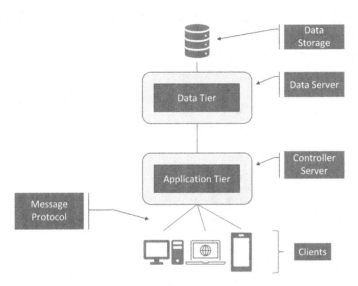

FIGURE 2.5
Extended Three-Tier Design

Service-Oriented Architecture

A Service-Oriented Architecture (SOA) extends an N-Tier Architecture by decomposing middle-tier (i.e., Controller) services into independent components. The best way to describe this design is by example.

Let's consider a typical web-based retail application. Conceptually, we can subdivide the purchase scenario as follows: product review, shopping cart interaction, and order placement. For this discussion, let's focus on the shopping cart abstraction.

Shopping carts provide several features. Users can:

- Request a cart (begin a purchase scenario)
- Add items to a cart
- Remove items from a cart
- Empty carts
- Return a cart (complete a purchase scenario)

Leveraging a three-tier design, we could incorporate these services into a single controller (as depicted in Figure 2.4). Alternatively, we could consider each service an individual component that clients may invoke independently. Figure 2.6 illustrates this approach.

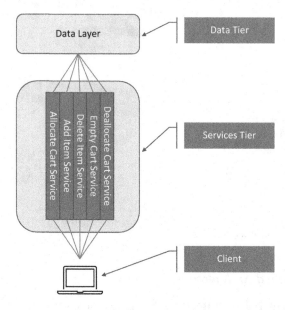

FIGURE 2.6
Example SOA Architecture

SOA is one of the most prevalent architectures in use today because the model allows independent service extension and maintenance. Moreover, developers can deploy new services with little disruption to those already in production.

Architectural Views

When building physical structures, blueprints document the architectural model and provide comprehensive construction plans. Despite being less tangible, IT architectures require a similar level of detail.

Although they can vary in format, a professional-caliber IT architecture should minimally include the following:

- A Context Diagram that presents the system in its environment. As depicted in Figure 2.7, this diagram should include users, system interfaces, and external connectivity.

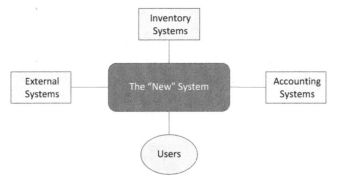

FIGURE 2.7
Example Context Diagram

- An Application Architecture Diagram. Often called a Container Diagram, this view presents the system's major software components. Figure 2.8 provides an example.

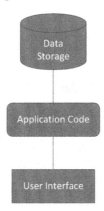

FIGURE 2.8
Example Application Architecture Diagram

- A Component Diagram. As depicted in Figure 2.9, this view presents

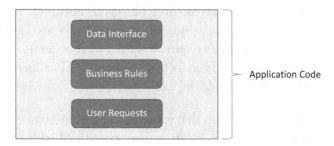

FIGURE 2.9
Example Component Diagram

the major modules within the Application Architecture.
- A Deployment Diagram depicts the configuration of system components. Figure 2.10 provides an example.

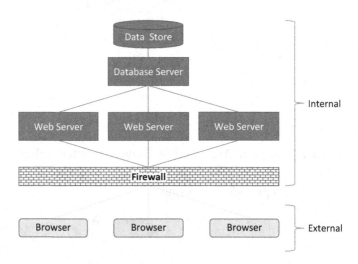

FIGURE 2.10
Example Deployment Diagram

- Figure 2.11 depicts a Data Flow Diagram. This view traces the flow of data as the system processes transactions.

FIGURE 2.11
Example Data Flow Diagram

- Professional IT architectures should also include a set of Architectural Principles that establish organizational values and guide all participants on how to fulfill the enterprise's mission. Each guideline should contain the following sections: a Name, the Declaration, a Justification, and Consequences (if any). Table 2.1 provides an example.

TABLE 2.1

Example Architectural Principles

Name	Business Continuity Guidelines
Declaration	The business must continue to operate at 95% capacity despite operational interruptions or technical failures.
Justification	One of the primary advantages we provide to our customers is reliability. Outages may cause customers to acquire services from another provider.
Consequences	All IT systems must be fault tolerant.

The preceding has been but a brief overview. As alluded to above, EAs use many other types of system diagrams to specify a complete solution. Nonetheless, the above architectural views should serve as a solid foundation for the following discussions.

Architectural Metrics

There are many metrics that can assess the effectiveness of an architecture. Some are obvious, but others are more subtle. Moreover, some benchmarks rely on the efficiency of the implementation. Thus, we can't always independently measure the quality of a design.

Nonetheless, there are still many effective methods by which we can evaluate the soundness of a proposed architecture. For reasons that will become obvious, we refer to these collectively as the "ilities."

However, I'd like to share two confessions before we discuss them.

Confession 4:

> Many Enterprise Architects don't consider quality attributes during the design phase.

Although I consider it highly unprofessional, many EAs become so concerned with meeting one or two critical requirements that they gloss over many others. And that's very unfortunate because faulty designs are often difficult to mitigate with code. Indeed, if not identified early, architectural flaws can wreak havoc and put many applications and projects at risk.

Confession 5:

> Enterprise Architects don't have the luxury of ignoring the "boring" or "trivial" aspects of a system or its design.

Enterprise Architects are responsible for a complete end-to-end design. Anything less is, in my opinion, unprofessional.

Enough said. Let's return to the benchmarks we use to evaluate architectural designs.

The sections that follow describe the most common design metrics. As you review this material, please remember that an Enterprise Architecture is all-encompassing, including servers, software, routers, switches, storage arrays, data standards, power supplies, etc. Thus, these metrics are all-encompassing. Consequently, EAs are (or should be) responsible for all design decisions. Finger-pointing and handwaves are unacceptable.

Availability   Expressed as a probability, Availability is a measure of the extent to which a system can process requests during specified service hours. This metric must account for all outages, including maintenance cycles, component servicing, software upgrades, and downtime caused by component failures.

So, for example, if the availability requirement is 99%, and the service window is 24 × 7 × 365, we can compute the system's total allowable downtime as follows:

Total minutes in a year: $60 \times 24 \times 365 = 525,600$

Total availability $525,600 \times 0.99 = 520,344$ minutes

Total permissible downtime $525,600 - 520,344 = 5,256$ minutes

Or only 87.6 hours (slightly more than two weeks) of permitted downtime for an entire year!

Please bear in mind that a 99% availability requirement is not considered aggressive by today's standards. Indeed, most systems should achieve 99.9% (i.e., "Three 9s") availability "out of the box." Moreover, most organizations expect systems to provide 99.99% ("Four 9s") availability, and some require 99.999%[4] ("Five 9s") uptime.

So, what's the moral of this little parable? EAs must consider Availability as a fundamental design element. It cannot be an afterthought.

Reliability   We define Reliability as the probability that a system will execute a given transaction

---

4 In the IT world, we usually express availability requirements by specifying the "number of 9s." For example, "three nines" means 99.9%, "four nines" means 99.99%, and "five nines" means 99.999%.

correctly within a specified performance requirement.

Many readers might be thinking, *We're dealing with computers. They're perfect, no?*

CPUs are highly accurate—close to perfect. However, many more hardware and software components are involved in transaction processing beyond the central processor: disk drives, network devices, and cabling—not to mention all the software developed by humans.

Moreover, the Reliability metric requires accurate results within a specified time. Thus, it's not enough that the system produces the correct result. It must also complete each transaction within the performance metric. This last bit makes the problem a bit more challenging.

Scalability   Scalability refers to how well a system responds to an increasing workload without impacting its performance. From an architectural viewpoint, Scalability refers to how easily we can expand system resources without affecting the user experience.

For example, we might ask questions such as:

- How many users can execute transactions concurrently?
- As we add more users, does application response time degrade?
- How does the system respond as users become more proficient and increase the transaction rate?

There are two main scaling strategies: Vertical and Horizontal. The first, Vertical Scaling, refers to the ability of system engineers to increase the horsepower of the underlying hardware. The more powerful the computer, the more workload the system can handle. Because this approach is essentially a purchase decision, it typically has no architectural implications.

Horizontal Scaling, however, is a function of the architecture because it refers to the system's ability to incorporate additional processing nodes and components without affecting transactional performance.

To highlight the differences between these approaches, consider two previously discussed architectural models. With a monolithic solution, our only choice is Vertical Scaling. However, a well-designed distributed architecture allows us to expand the system by adding servers/components to each layer.

Elasticity   Related to Scalability, Elasticity refers to a system's ability to respond to workload variations via an automated provisioning and de-provisioning process.[5]

In other words, the system self-monitors its transaction rate. As the workload increases, it adds servers (from a pool of available processors) and relinquishes them as the load decreases.

This capability requires architectural support and is commonplace in modern cloud computing solutions.

Extensibility   An architecture's Extensibility reflects the effort required to expand or modify a system's functionality post-deployment. In

---

5 This is sometimes called *Dynamic Scalability*.

other words, it's a measure of how easily an application can accommodate change.

Unfortunately, unlike the other metrics discussed in this section, we can apply no empirical measures to evaluate a design's extensibility. Instead, we must consider characteristics such as:

- Flexibility: The ability of a system to accommodate additional functionality and adapt to changes in the business environment.
- Configurability: Systems should accommodate change through configuration rather than programming. In other words, change parameters, not code.
- Interoperability: Applications should easily integrate with other infrastructure components. To put it another way, systems should "play nice" in the enterprise sandbox.

Performance[6]   Regardless of the breadth of its functionality, a system that does not appear responsive will remain unused. Most users frustrate easily. EAs should therefore ensure their designs meet or exceed performance requirements.

However, responsiveness is subjective. For example, one person's "acceptable" is another individual's "way too slow." Thus, performance requirements must define objective, testable specifications, such as:

The system shall execute all transactions in 0.75 seconds 97% of the time under a maximum load of 2,000 concurrent users.

---

6 In keeping with the notion of "ilities," maybe I should have called this attribute "Performab*ility*"?

Testability   Stated simply, Testability measures the ease by which we can verify a system's adherence to requirements—both as a whole and its constituent components.

Many factors affect testability, including:

- Transparency: How well the internal design and implementation are exposed to test engineers
- Clarity: Are all system requirements expressed clearly and without ambiguity
- Specification: How accurate is the system documentation
- Comprehensiveness: How much of the system gets tested

One measure of component testability is code coverage. Test engineers try to ensure that every line of code has been verified. Unfortunately, this is not always possible or practical.

WHAT IS ENTERPRISE ARCHITECTURE?

Now that we have an overview of IT architecture, let's dive a bit deeper and refine our model of Enterprise Architecture.

Before we begin, however, please recall the caveat noted in Chapter 1: This is NOT a formal, comprehensive treatise on EA. Thus, I've included this material to provide a conceptual foundation for those readers who might not have a technical background.

Municipal Planning Board

Although not perfect, we can draw upon a familiar example that can serve as a metaphor for Enterprise Architecture: A municipal planning board.

Most municipal planning boards hold many responsibilities, such as:

- Formulating and managing a Town Vision
- Establishing and administrating a Zoning Plan
- Defining and enforcing a set of Building Codes
- Identifying and preserving Legacy Buildings

Collectively, these tasks establish a vision for the town's future, identify specific goals, and define a set of strategies to achieve them. We can relate the obligations of a planning board to the objectives of an Enterprise Architecture.

Town Vision   All organizations (municipal, commercial, philanthropic, etc.) should establish a strategic plan that defines and codifies long-term objectives, guiding all future development and providing a framework for all tactical initiatives. As we will discuss below, Organizational Governance and Business Architecture serve this purpose in Enterprise Architecture.

Zoning Plan   A Zoning Plan serves as a roadmap that guides a municipality's growth and development. For example, city planners might establish rules specifying that "industrial parks" may not reside within a mile of a school. Or they might designate certain sections of the town as "residential" and restrict the types of commercial enterprises within those zones. This Enterprise Architecture equivalent is an Infrastructure Architecture that establishes deployment guidelines.

Building Codes   Municipal Building Codes specify the processes, materials, and best practices when constructing or remodeling a building. The equivalent in Enterprise Architecture is a set of standards, certified technologies, and approved methodologies to which all application development must adhere.

Historic Preservation	Most communities like to maintain links to their past. Preserving buildings of historical significance is one way of achieving that goal. IT shops have similar concerns—except that the focus centers on leveraging prior investment and minimizing environmental "churn." Thus, an Enterprise Architecture might designate certain applications as "off-limits" when environments undergo a refresh.

Note that nowhere in the prior discussion did we state that town planners must (or even should) specify the architecture of individual buildings. That is not within their purview. For example, in a residential area, an owner may build a house of any type on a vacant lot: cape cod, center hall colonial, contemporary ranch, etc. The point is that the architectures of those structures are independent and, when appropriate, unique. Nonetheless, regardless of its design, every building must adhere to all the requirements and guidelines specified by the Zoning Board.

Similarly, this approach should apply to Enterprise Architecture. That is, although all applications should adhere to the Enterprise Architecture's standards, methodologies, and best practices (e.g., minimal availability, performance metrics, and approved technologies), Application Architects should be free to adopt a design that best serves their users' needs.[7]

There are some caveats and considerations, however.

Confession 6:

Despite what some architects profess, the newest technology is not necessarily the best choice.

Though customizing the design of individual applications has many advantages, IT shops cannot countenance a technological "free-for-all." There are many benefits to using proven technology, including:

---

7 At least, in my opinion. I've worked with some Enterprise Architects who oppose this position.

"Tried and True"	Existing solutions are well-integrated into the enterprise infrastructure
"The Devil You Know"	Leveraging existing tools minimizes surprises late in the SDLC
Organization Consistency	Reusing technologies limits the number of products, support issues, licenses, and skillsets an organization must manage and maintain

Unfortunately, "new" has a nice shine to it.

Confession 7:

> Many Application Architects feel they must "strut their stuff" by including the "latest and greatest" technologies in their designs.

Whether it's to pad their resumes or demonstrate that they read industry journals, many Application Architects are not content unless they are standing near the bleeding edge of technology. Sadly, these "enlightened" individuals remain blissfully unaware of the organizational implications of designs that deviate from "the norm."

For example, consider the following concerns associated with adopting a one-off technology for an application:

- Does the current staff have the appropriate knowledge and experience to use it?
- What are the licensing fees?
- Does the product integrate well with the rest of the environment?
- If adopted, can other applications leverage the new product?
- Does the vendor have long-term viability?

Although they are common—and sometimes even appropriate— deviations from Enterprise Architecture standards should require justification, review, and approval. (More on this later in the chapter.)

We will return to the above discussion points in different contexts later in the text.

So, What's Enterprise Architecture?

Thus far, we've spiraled around an explanation of Enterprise Architecture. I think it's time we steer toward the center.

As is often the case, a definition is an excellent place to start.

Definition 3:

Enterprise Architecture is a holistic blueprint that stakeholders can use to plan, govern, design, build, and deploy solutions in a cohesive manner that meets and furthers an organization's goals.

There are several items to note concerning this definition.

First, Enterprise Architecture serves as an organization's blueprint, and to some folks, that implies a level of rigidity or inflexibility. On the contrary, that should never be the case; exceptions are as regular as the seasons—though far more frequent. Thus, an Enterprise Architecture should accommodate deviations and provide formal pathways for their inclusion.

Next, let's discuss the term "solution." Many folks assume that an Enterprise Architecture encompasses only "homegrown applications."

Au contraire, mon ami.

That should never be the case. There are many advantages to a heterogeneous solution landscape that integrates in-house development, purchased products, and customized applications (i.e., modified third-party systems). A professional-caliber Enterprise Architecture should accommodate technical diversity.

Finally, the objective of any Enterprise Architecture is to serve the organization's needs. That is, it's not a self-sustaining, standalone entity. Instead, like development shops in general, Enterprise Architecture provides the infrastructure upon which the rest of the organization runs: it's the track, not the train.[8] Stakeholders decide what the business needs; the IT department builds it.

---

8 This analogy does not necessarily hold true for development organizations like IBM, Microsoft, and Google, whose primary product is application software. Obviously, for such companies, software is their *raison d'être*.

That is not to say that every development shop is simply a wagged tail. On the contrary, technologists should actively contribute and suggest solutions and alternatives to decision-makers. But once stakeholders have established a direction, the IT team must develop an Enterprise Architecture that leads the organization along the intended path.

Why Is Enterprise Architecture Important?

The remainder of this chapter—indeed, this entire text—focuses on the importance of Enterprise Architecture. However, as a preview, the following list summarizes its significance in supporting modern, large-scale system development.

Enterprise Architecture:

- Allows stakeholders to make informed decisions regarding *change*
- Records and memorializes technical decisions (as captured in various artifacts)
- Establishes boundaries and principles governing application design
- Reflects the structure and goals of an organization
- Defines a reusable design model suitable for (most) applications
- Facilitates the interoperability and integration of third-party tools and systems
- Centralizes essential design elements (e.g., security)
- Enables Application Architects to focus on solutions rather than technologies

Major Enterprise Architectural Elements

As noted previously, there are several types of IT architectures that, collectively, comprise a complete enterprise solution. More formally, we can group these designs—and their corresponding views—into a framework that forms a comprehensive Enterprise Architecture.

Although simplified, Figure 2.12 depicts the major components of an Enterprise Architecture Framework.

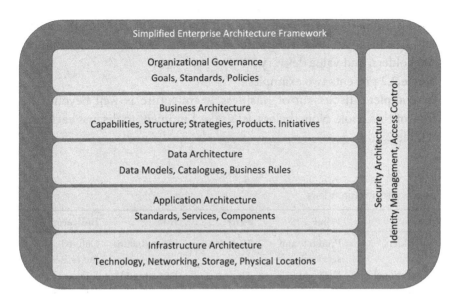

FIGURE 2.12
Simplified Enterprise Architecture Framework

Organizational Governance

At the top of the diagram rests Organizational Governance, which represents the senior executives who set policy and direction. Although their approach might not be as formal as subsequent layers, their decisions have sweeping consequences for the organization.

However, senior executives can't—and shouldn't—operate in a vacuum. They require timely, accurate, and reliable information to have the best chance of making informed decisions that benefit the organization.

Business Architecture

That leads us to the first structured layer, Business Architecture (BA), which serves as the blueprint for the entire organization.

Definition 4:

Business Architecture defines an organization's current and future state and specifies the transition plan to achieve its objectives.

Using comprehensive views (and their relationships), BA is a discipline that specifies an organization's structure, strategies, capabilities, stakeholders, and value delivery.

Table 2.2 presents two examples.

A complete discussion of Business Architecture is well beyond the scope of this book. Nonetheless, let's take a moment to discuss each row in Table 2.2.

TABLE 2.2

Business Architecture Views

Who	What	Why	How	Indicators
Stakeholders	Products and services	Vision	Value streams	Defined metrics
Organizational structure	Data and information	Strategies	Projects and directives	Industry standards

Row 1 centers on the organization's Vision, its Stakeholders, and the Products and Services provided by the enterprise. The term, Value Streams, denotes tasks (actions and activities)[9] that benefit patrons.[10]

Row 2 focuses on structures, including *organigrams*,[11] data organization, strategies (as concrete manifestations of the Vision), and projects that direct the efforts and resources of an enterprise.

Please note that each row also includes a column for indicators and metrics. This is because defining an objective is problematic without establishing a metric by which stakeholders can measure accomplishment. Otherwise, there is no way to assess progress. Thus, as a rule, Business Architects should establish *quantifiable* success criteria for all tasks, objectives, and goals.

Data Architecture

The next level of Enterprise Architecture, just below Business Architecture, is Data Architecture.

---

9 The tasks may be manual, automated, or both.

10 I use the nonstandard term "patrons" because for some enterprises (e.g., charitable foundations), the beneficiaries of an organization's tasks might not be "customers."

11 i.e., "Org Charts."

Definition 5:

Data Architecture defines the structure, tools, and standards that govern the collection, organization, and availability of enterprise data.

Data, and its processed equivalent information, are the crown jewels of the modern enterprise. Consider how few applications you've used—personally or professionally—that haven't leveraged some centralized data store.

Please pause to reflect on this point.

Other than some standalone games (e.g., Chess and Sudoku) that might use pseudo-random number generators to establish an initial state, few applications operate without engaging in some form of data manipulation. It can be as simple as saving state (e.g., storing items placed in a shopping cart until checkout) to the sophisticated queries of a data scientist trying to predict the voting trends of millennials.

When structured and organized correctly, data drives decisions, facilitates operations, and spurs innovation. It is also an asset that many organizations can leverage and monetize as an independent revenue stream.

Due to its enterprise-wide significance, we cannot leave data modeling to individual Application Architects who, by necessity, must adopt a narrow focus. Thus, Data Architecture deserves its prominent status within an Enterprise Architecture.

Application Architecture

Positioned below Data Architecture in the framework hierarchy is Application Architecture. This topic is likely to be the most familiar aspect of Enterprise Architecture for most readers because it embodies the most common and traditional elements of system design.

As mentioned earlier in this chapter, Application Architecture specifies the design, technologies, and tools used to develop systems and components. Furthermore, Application Architects must address additional aspects such as programming language selections, reusable components, buy-vs-build decisions, and testing tools.

Most notably, this is the point where architecture transitions to design. However, due to the subtleties involved, we'll postpone this discussion until later in the text.

Infrastructure Architecture

Serving as the foundational layer of the framework is Infrastructure Architecture.[12] Unfortunately, this term holds various interpretations in the current literature. However, below is a definition that I'm comfortable with and seems to be gaining traction in the industry.

Definition 6:

> Infrastructure Architecture specifies the structure, organization, and design of low-level hardware components.

Generally speaking, the Infrastructure Architecture addresses the following design elements:

Data Centers	Physical locations, power supplies, business continuity concerns, cloud vendor selection, etc.
Hardware	Servers, end-user devices (when purchased and supported by the organization), disk arrays, etc.
Components	Operating systems, change management systems, software deployment tools, etc.
Networking	Routers, switches, firewalls, etc. Note that many organizations specify these designs in a standalone Network Architecture.

---

12 To help *confuse* the issue, Infrastructure Architecture is also called Technical Architecture.

Security Architecture

Unfortunately, we live in an age of hackers, piracy, and ransomware. As a result, organizations must implement adequate precautions to protect their digital assets and prevent interruption to their business. Thus, cutting across all aspects of an Enterprise Architecture is the Security Architecture.

Confession 8:

> Security Architects are delighted to tell you what you *shouldn't* do but rarely instruct you on what you *should* do.

Alas, it's been my experience that Security Architects rarely guide an organization's security measures and are loath to suggest solutions. Usually, it falls upon the Enterprise and Application Architects to repeatedly propose designs until the security team does not reject one.

Talk about the tail wagging the dog.

We will return to this point later in the text.

Value Proposition

To the dismay of many IT professionals, more often than not, it's distinctly counterproductive to allow Application Architects to have free reign over their designs.

Confession 9:

> Application Architects are wont to gripe *ad nauseam* about adopting a cookie-cutter approach to design and the lack of forethought and missed opportunities when stakeholders reject the inclusion of new technologies.

As alluded to earlier in this chapter, Application Architects believe that being forced to adhere to an Enterprise Architecture stifles their creativity and prevents them from developing optimal designs for their systems. Indeed, the griping is often incessant, and it can become the bane of an

Enterprise Architect's existence. (Well, that and Business Analysts—but we'll return to this point in a later chapter.)

Unfortunately, given their (appropriately) narrow perspective, Application Architects often remain blissfully unaware of some critical enterprise concerns, such as:

- Every new technology adopted by a development shop:
  - Requires product-specific knowledge—The organization must hire staff (development, testing, deployment, and maintenance) to support every new component it integrates into its applications and infrastructure
  - Increases licensing costs—A site license for an enterprise Database Management System (DBMS) is likely less expensive than the sum cost of multiple application-specific database products
  - Complicates integration efforts—Integrating data sets across individual applications that employ diverse database technologies is typically more complicated than using one centralized data store
- Unique designs for each application:
  - Reduces staff fungibility—Product knowledge (or the lack thereof) hinders developers' ability to support multiple applications
  - Thwarts component reuse—Developers may find that some software libraries do not lend themselves to all environments
  - Imposes deployment issues—As you expand the number of products in use across the infrastructure, you also increase the likelihood of having to create one-off deployment scripts
- All tools/products/libraries must:
  - Adhere to enterprise security requirements—Each new tool or library adopted increases vetting efforts and the potential vulnerabilities
  - Include professional support from a reputable vendor—Organizations can't gamble on whether some shaky startup will be viable for the duration of a critical product's entire lifecycle
  - Undergo functional and performance testing—Organizations should never take vendors at their word regarding the robustness of their products. To paraphrase a former president: Trust but verify

There are many more enterprise concerns, but this will suffice for our purposes.

As I mentioned previously, this is not a tome on Enterprise Architecture. Nonetheless, the point is that Enterprise Architecture brings order to the chaos—admittedly, this is not without its own set of costs and exceptions. (More on this later.)

To hone this idea, we can express the Value Proposition of Enterprise Architecture as follows:

Values   This attribute is not the sole province of the Human Resources department. How an organization implements its solutions reflects its culture and values. Enterprise Architecture formalizes this for the IT shop.

Principles   Architecture Principles serve to establish and memorialize an organization's governing standards and priorities. Yes, they may change. (What doesn't?) But while they remain illuminated, they serve as beacons that guide all IT endeavors.

Governance   Enterprise Architecture serves as the who, what, where, and how of IT. It ensures that the appropriate stakeholders remain informed, undertake the required due diligence and analysis, and disseminate policy decisions as necessary.

Management   Change happens. (I'll spare you the usual litany of cheesy clichés.) The critical point is that Enterprise Architecture allows senior stakeholders to understand the business impacts and technical implications of 'forced evolution' (i.e., changes required due to external forces such as market fluctuations) and arrive at informed decisions.

Agency   Is your current IT architecture a result of deliberate actions in pursuit of organizationally defined goals or a hodge-podge amalgamation of one-off choices? Enterprise Architecture *drives* technical decisions; it's not a passenger.

At this point, I'm sure some readers are taking exception to the fact that I have not discussed any exceptions. Obviously, not every aspect of life—or technical design—falls neatly into cookie-cutter categories. As a result, some systems will not align with every specification of an Enterprise Architecture.

For example, the architectural design of your Data Lake might not look exactly like that of your Order Management System. But that's okay; it shouldn't.

The point is that, with an Enterprise Architecture in place, senior stakeholders remain in control. They review and approve all proposed exceptions and decide how far they may deviate from the "norm." Moreover, through the application of formal design techniques, they can ensure that all such "anomalous applications" still "play nicely in the sandbox."

One last comment on exceptions. It's been my experience that the 80/20 rule applies here. Eighty percent of homegrown systems will align nicely with the Enterprise Architecture, given a reasonably decent design, allowing architects to focus their efforts on the remaining 20%.

Costs and ROI

Developing and managing an Enterprise Architecture is a project in its own right. It minimally requires an Enterprise Architect (EA)—but that's just the proverbial tip of the iceberg. Depending on the organization's size, an EA may require technical and administrative support staff.

There are other costs as well.

During project startup, EAs will conduct due diligence to ascertain the current state of the enterprise, which will necessitate numerous interviews with various stakeholders: programmers, designers, support staff, users, etc. As you might expect, this task will impact participants' productivity.

After completing the due diligence effort, the architecture team will need time to develop and disseminate their proposed design. This task usually entails a series of "dog and pony shows" targeted to various stakeholder segments.

Once the proposed Enterprise Architecture has received approval, the EA must review all future designs to ensure conformance: network modifications, application architectures, data models, etc. These evaluations may impact project schedules and costs (both positively and negatively).

So, how do you know whether developing an Enterprise Architecture is beneficial, given the above investment?

Below are *tangible* evaluation criteria to compute an expected Return on Investment (ROI).

- Savings on licensing fees
- Reduced cost/effort/time for system integration
- Shorter overall development cycles
- Smaller development staffs
- Smaller infrastructure footprint

But the advantages of adopting an EA are not limited to the above quantifiable benefits. Other, less tangible considerations include:

- Improved user experience
- Faster response to changing business needs
- Increased reliability/fewer outages
- Development staff fungibility

Pro Tip 2:

When talking to the "number crunchers," emphasize that developing an Enterprise Architecture won't instantly help the bottom line.

The ROI for an Enterprise Architecture is not immediate. However, after a year or two, it will positively impact the costs and culture of any organization.

ENTERPRISE ARCHITECTURE IN PRACTICE

To understand the benefits of Enterprise Architecture in practice, let's begin by leveraging the ideas expressed by the two quotes appearing at the beginning of this chapter.

Confession 10:

Enterprise Architecture is about *change.*

Enterprise Architecture is not about adopting the newest framework, incorporating the slickest technologies, or meeting the needs of the squeakiest wheel in an organization. On the contrary, Enterprise Architecture is about designing a flexible framework and a pliable infrastructure that can accommodate change.

As you may have already noticed, beginning with Chapter 1, change—or, more specifically, *accommodating change*—will be a recurring theme throughout this book.

Confession 11:

Accommodating change is the sole constant in the professional life of an Enterprise Architect.

Yes, despite my earlier promise, Confession 11 contains a tired cliché. However, platitudes of this nature become overused because of their inherent verity.

Thus, despite its triteness, this principle cannot be overstated. If it only addresses today's needs, even the slickest of Enterprise Architectures will be riddled with hacks and workarounds tomorrow. It's as inevitable as the inexorable march of time.

But good architectural design is not just about instituting rules. It's also about not constructing impediments.

Confession 12:

Enterprise Architecture must enable interoperability and extension.

Consider a personal computer (PC) designed without any interfaces: no ports, peripherals, or external connections other than a power chord. Let's further assume that we've installed the device in a secured location that requires three forms of biometric input, two passwords, and one note from your mother to gain entry.

Is that computer safe?

It would undoubtedly rank among the most secure devices in existence.

Is that PC useful?

I think we'd all agree that the answer to that question is: Not in any practical sense.

The point is that because computers must interoperate with some portion of the world, security is among the most critical design aspects of modern IT architecture. Yet, it cannot be so restrictive as to prohibit users from gaining access to essential systems. Otherwise, it's a self-defeating proposition.

Similarly, an Enterprise Architecture cannot be so inflexible that it hinders extension. Instead, its design must encourage expansion and integration.

I'm not exaggerating when I state that new devices, tools, and computing models find their way into the marketplace daily. Therefore, the ability of an organization to remain competitive may rest on the capability of its Enterprise Architecture to incorporate new products, systems, and technologies. Thus, Enterprise Architects must make extensibility a primary design concern.

Unfortunately, extensibility is not the only significant design attribute EAs address after the fact.

Confession 13:

> System performance is often an afterthought for many Enterprise Architects.

Sadly, performance—among many other "ilities" discussed above—is often a secondary consideration. Instead, many EAs focus on one or two business priorities while losing sight of other essential design elements. Such omissions are costly to mitigate when identified late in the project lifecycle.

Confession 14:

> Many Enterprise Architects forget that data is the most valuable asset of any organization.

As discussed above, an enterprise data model might be the most valuable IT artifact in any organization. Unfortunately, I've worked with many Enterprise Architects who are not conversant with the discipline of data modeling and therefore leave that task to others.

Now, I'm not suggesting that EAs shouldn't rely on the expertise of experienced data modelers. What I am suggesting, however, is that Enterprise Architects should be "elbows deep" in the design of the organization's Data Architecture.

Confession 15:

Many IT designers—not just architects—forget that simplicity counts.

Occam's Razor Rules—or should.

When confronted with a flaw in one of their designs, I can't tell you how many times I've witnessed architects simply "add another box" to a drawing. These lazy charlatans forget or are ignorant of the fact that every added component requires:

- Designing
- Development
- Testing
- Security evaluations
- Deployment
- Maintenance

Every such "hand wave" has a price tag that is way too costly to ignore.

SUMMARY

This chapter was but a brief overview of several topics, all of which deserve a dedicated chapter—if not an entire book. Nonetheless, although not as thorough as the subject matter deserves, I believe that, in broad strokes, we've painted a picture of Enterprise Architecture that would otherwise require multiple canvases.

We began the chapter by defining IT architecture, discussing its various types, and reviewing the standard models. Then, based on that foundation, we defined Enterprise Architecture, its significant elements, and how it's most often applied in practice.

Next up: We'll examine the role of the Enterprise Architect in detail.

And, of course, more ranting.

3

The Role of an Enterprise Architect

The difference between good and bad architecture is the time you spend on it.

—David Chipperfield

As an architect, you design for the present with an awareness of the past for a future which is essentially unknown.

—Norman Foster

INTRODUCTION

Ever since *Homo sapiens* started building things, individuals have served as architects. For example, some early humans learned the best way to pile rocks or stack blocks of ice to form a stable shelter.

As people began residing in one place for extended periods, the structures became more permanent and, therefore, more solid. Early construction materials like branches and animal hides would eventually yield to longer-lasting natural resources such as clay and timber, which, in turn, were supplanted by human-created products like bricks and metal.

But the evolution didn't end there.

As societies formed, people learned the benefits of sharing the burdens of life. As a result, they would identify individuals who had developed specialized skills to undertake important jobs on behalf of entire groups.

DOI: 10.1201/9781003414285-3

When it came to construction, this led to the role of the modern-day architect.

This progression has continued into the technological era leading to the advent of the Enterprise Architect (EA). This chapter will review the EA's roles[1] and responsibilities and understand how they fit and function within a modern development shop.

Before we begin, however, I'd like to share one caveat. Because many readers may have skipped Chapter 2, I will reiterate a few confessions. Indeed, some of them are worthy of repetition.

WHY DO WE NEED ARCHITECTS?

Unfortunately, these days you can't seem to swing a lifeless leonine without hitting someone who adorns their title with the word "Architect." Consequently, stakeholders have grown wary of anyone sporting such an honorific—and rightly so because it's often a self-proclaimed title rather than an earned credential.

Confession 1:

> Many architectural roles are not fully understood by stakeholders (or other architects, for that matter).

Thus, it would seem sensible and prudent to understand what architects do. Or *should* do. To that end, let's begin with a practical description of the essential architectural roles and how they evolved in the world of IT.

One caveat: At the time of this writing, there are no standards in the literature for the role names and no convergence regarding their specific responsibilities. That said, the following descriptions conform with the definitions typically used by practicing professionals; thus, we will use them throughout this book.

---

1 Yes, I used the plural for "roles." We'll see why shortly.

Unwieldy Applications	When applications become cumbersome and complicated, development teams need someone to bring order to the chaos. Depending on the size and complexity of a given project, we would assign this task to a **Lead Developer** or an **Application Architect**. The individual assuming this responsibility must set technical direction, refine/revise the design, and ensure conformance with organizational requirements, guidelines, and principles.
Infrastructure Components	As an organization grows, its reliance on hardware platforms and networking components multiplies. As this complexity increases, development shops often require the full-time attention of a **Systems Architect** to manage the demands of expanding infrastructure.
Application Profusion	As the number of development projects increases, it becomes progressively difficult for Application and System Architects to ensure strategic alignment among applications and their associated infrastructure. As a result, IT shops often employ Solution Architects to address issues holistically in such cases.
Business Goals	When the development landscape broadens, an organization's technological foundation often diverges from its strategic goals. Enter the role of **Enterprise Architect**, whose responsibilities include defining and coordinating the efforts of all the other architects involved in large-scale system development and ensuring conformance with organizational policy.

Data Organization	As I've already mentioned, data is an organization's most critical technical resource. As such, it deserves the full-time attention of an expert. Hence the need for a **Data Architect.**
Business Strategy	In the growing discipline of Business Architecture, **Business Architects** help craft and codify business strategies and capabilities using artifacts such as Capability Maps and Value Streams.

The above list is by no means comprehensive. For example, some of the literature argues that Information Architects, Platform Architects, and Deployment Architects also play essential roles in modern system design.

I do not.

To me, such appellations describe *tasks*, not *professions*. Moreover, it's unclear how these roles distinguish themselves from those described above.

To further my point, let's examine the terms "construction" and "development." We often use these words interchangeably, but they are not equivalent.[2]

For example, as I alluded to in the opening paragraphs of this chapter, architects participate in the *construction* of things. However, we use the term *development* when referring to programmers writing software.

Why is this so, you might ask?

Because buildings don't *develop*, that is, once built, they stay, well, built.[3]

And we don't *construct* software programs because—as all of us in this industry are painfully aware—they are never complete. They get extended, replaced, retired, or become too risky to revise. However, as long as they remain functional and "online," applications will always have a backlog of bugs, technical debt, and a punch list of pending change requests.

Thus, anyone who modifies an automated process, extends an application's functionality, or revises a piece of code is not engaging in anything remotely "architectural." In contrast, artifacts produced by anyone with the title "architect" must culminate in some sort of *construction*—even if the items they design are not tangible.

---

2 Please visit the Worldwide Institute of Software Architects for a more thorough discussion of this topic.

3 As a rule. Yes, you can add extensions to existing structures.

To be clear, I'm not suggesting that one task or role is more significant than any other. Instead, I'm railing against the indiscriminate use of the term "architect" because it diminishes the title's significance and confuses stakeholders.

Now that I've gotten that rant off my chest, let's consider what Enterprise Architects do.

WHAT ARE THE ATTRIBUTES OF AN ENTERPRISE ARCHITECT?

I'm sure everyone who has worked on a large-scale development project would agree that it is not a simple undertaking. There are usually scores of stakeholders (way too many if you ask me, but we'll return to this point later in the text), hundreds (if not thousands) of requirements, and more wavering opinions than one hears uttered from a podium in a political debate. And, of course, let us not omit the naïve and inflexible budgets, the unrealistic can't-possibly-slip schedules, and the all-consuming fear of change that can paralyze even the most determined advocates.

At the center of this maelstrom stands the Enterprise Architect, whose job is to curtail the chaos, tame the tumult, and manage the mayhem.

Confession 2:

> Many Enterprise Architects cannot cope with the vortex of confusion synonymous with system development.

Projects—even large ones—begin at a pedestrian pace: Requirements defined, business objectives identified, and personnel selected. Then, one day without warning, the wind starts swirling, ominous clouds darken the sky, and thunderstorms deluge all hope of success.

Confession 3:

> Regardless of culpability, Enterprise Architects serve as the lightning rod for every "bolt from the blue."

Let me share some real examples with you that, as an Enterprise Architect, I had to address.

- A third-party database interface library didn't integrate well with the organization's legacy Database Management System (DBMS) despite the vendor's promises to the contrary.
- System testing halted because the newly acquired automation tool could not "drive" the existing User Interface (UI) framework.
- The users expressed unhappiness with the UI layouts, requiring a redesign of the entire suite of wireframes.

You may well be wondering whether any of the above issues are architectural.

I assure you they are not. But, from a practical perspective, the point is moot.

In most development shops (admittedly, there are exceptions), all eyes focus on the Enterprise Architect when the fecal matter starts flying. As a result, regardless of their architectural implications, it's the EA that must suggest/uncover/devise the means to mitigate most project-related issues. Not always, but often.

That said, for better or worse, EAs should consider this task a job requirement and get on with it.

Confession 4:

> Many Enterprise Architects actively avoid difficult decisions.

As an Enterprise Architect, you need to "step up" because the "buck stops" with you. You're the individual who must select a "way forward" from alternatives that are frequently complex, conflicting, confusing, and often less than copacetic.

That said, EAs shouldn't feel compelled to fly solo. Indeed, they can—and should—rely on advice, suggestion, and research. Nonetheless, if you're an individual who can't remain self-possessed amid such turbulence, then maybe you should consider choosing a more tranquil flight plan for your career.

However, if you decide to stick it out, the material below will discuss additional responsibilities you'll need to assume. But, before we drill down on the EA's duties, let's begin with a definition of the role that loosely aligns with the current literature.

Definition 1:

An Enterprise Architect is an expert technologist who works with key stakeholders to develop a strategy to manage an organization's IT infrastructure, investments, and assets.

Let's begin parsing this definition with the word "expert." Wiktionary defines this term as:

Definition 2:

An *expert* is an individual with extensive knowledge or capability in a subject.

That's all well and good. However, a professional Enterprise Architect cannot be an expert in a single subject. Instead, EAs must be highly accomplished in numerous disciplines and extremely conversant in many others (see below).

Confession 5:

Many Enterprise Architects are one-trick ponies.

When I assert that Enterprise Architects must possess expertise across many specialties, I don't mean in a "jack of all trades, master of none" sense of the term. On the contrary, the EA must possess detailed knowledge across many disciplines—not all of them technical (as we'll see.)

For example, if a project's Data Architect proposes a design change affecting the normalization of a critical data set, the Enterprise Architect must:

- Understand the potential implications of the proposed modification (technical, architectural, schedule, budgetary, etc.)
- Assess the relative advantages/disadvantages for the enterprise (e.g., Do the long-term benefits outweigh any short-term ramifications?)
- If adopted, alert all affected stakeholders (e.g., Application Architects, Test Teams, Project Managers, etc.) of the impending change and provide them with individualized impact assessments

In this example, an informed decision is unlikely if the Enterprise Architect lacks proficiency in data normalization, scheduling issues, budgetary concerns, and the technical constraints of affected development teams.

Returning to Definition 1, the term "stakeholders" refers to any members of the following groups:

- Senior Executives who establish the organization's vision
- Subject Matter Experts (SMEs) (both in-house and outside) in fields ranging from marketing to technology
- Project Architects from various disciplines (e.g., Business, Data, etc.), as described previously
- Developers and implementors (from programmers to network engineers) who will "stand up" the completed designs
- Users who will interact with completed applications
- Any others who can contribute or benefit to/from the project

Confession 6:

> Many Enterprise Architects don't have the self-confidence to admit when they lack pertinent expertise.

Enterprise Architects must have strong personalities and an internal drive worthy of their convictions. (Assuming they have any.) Moreover, EAs can't let the inhibitions of a fragile ego cause them to become tentative about asking for help. EAs must do what's best for the enterprise.
Period.

Confession 7:

A *professional* Enterprise Architect learns on the job.

No one is born educated; like experience, knowledge is acquired. Thus, no one—including Enterprise Architects—should ever feel too embarrassed to say, "I don't know."[4]

Nevertheless, whenever they believe they lack depth or breadth in a requisite discipline, *professional* EAs must immediately and thoroughly remedy their ignorance by undertaking any or all of the following tasks:

- Attend conferences and seminars
- Read books
- Speak with colleagues
- Search the Web (although one must be wary when relying on information acquired in this manner)

Confession 8:

In addition to being One-Trick Ponies (Confession 5), many Enterprise Architects are lazy.

As noted above, ignorance is an innate characteristic of the human condition. Apathy, on the other hand, is a choice.

Although this comment might reveal a character flaw on my part, the fact is I have no respect for any self-proclaimed Enterprise Architect who refuses to overcome an acknowledged lack of knowledge.

Sorry, not sorry.

For true professionals, remaining uninformed is not an option. Thus, if you call yourself an Enterprise Architect, then ignorance is not bliss.

---

4 This exoneration does NOT apply to foundational knowledge *assumed* in any profession. For example, accountants must understand debits and credits, programmers must understand iteration and selection, and IT architects must understand essential design models like MVC and SOA. End of story.

Confession 9:

> Many Enterprise Architects lack common sense.

I'm not a psychologist, so I cannot wax philosophic on whether common sense is a consequence of nature or nurture—or a combination of both. I just know that some folks have it, and others don't.

Enterprise Architects that lack this quality are working at a disadvantage. Again, sorry, not sorry.

Okay, let's move on. As I stated earlier, Enterprise Architects must possess a broad range of knowledge and abilities. So let's look more closely at what that means.

Although the categories are somewhat arbitrary, we can classify the requisite skillsets of an Enterprise Architect as listed below. Please note, however, this is not an exhaustive list, nor will I expound on every topic.

Strategy Development

Formulating a Technological Vision

Formulating a Technological Vision might be the most crucial skill an Enterprise Architect brings to the party. In effect, this task places a stake in the ground that serves as a guidepost for all subsequent activities involved in system development.

Confession 10:

> Many Enterprise Architects lack the capacity, disposition, desire, or determination to establish a technological vision.

Pro Tip 1:

> An Enterprise Architect should establish a guidepost even if it has to move rather than leaving the development team directionless.

Technology anarchy ensues when Enterprise Architects leave developers to their own devices. The resulting chaos is not a result of some conspiracy or a concerted attempt to thwart success. It's just human nature.

Developing an Enterprise Architecture

Developing an Enterprise Architecture is the *raison d'être* of the Enterprise Architect. In practical terms, it is the codification of the Technological Vision.

Confession 11:

> You would be dismayed to discover how many Enterprise Architects lack the skills to develop and Enterprise Architecture.

This point hearkens back to my comment concerning the arbitrary nature by which some individuals assume the title architect.

Formulating a Transition Plan

Unless you're developing in a greenfield,[5] every organization has a "current state." Thus, it's usually the case that one of the EA's most essential deliverables is a plan that will guide an organization's transition from its "as is" state to the new architectural vision.

This effort should include analyzing all existing applications to determine which get retired, replaced, or upgraded.

Confession 12:

> Many Enterprise Architects give short shrift to an organization's Transition Plan.

---

5 The term *greenfield* began in the construction industry. It refers to any construction site without any existing buildings on it. Thus, there is no need to raze any existing structures to make way for the new ones. In IT, the term refers to any new projects that are not replacing or integrating with any existing systems.

This task is not trivial and requires more than a "handwave." In addition, a thorough understanding of an organization's goals and vision is a prerequisite for developing a transition plan (see below).

Required Areas of Expertise

Understanding the Business

This task/skill is so basic that you may think it's too obvious to state. *Au contraire, mon ami!*

Confession 13:

> Many Enterprise Architects believe they need not concern themselves with such mundane considerations as an organization's goals and vision.

One cannot overstate the importance of this effort. Like accountants, Enterprise Architects must understand the enterprise and its business before recommending sweeping changes.

Architecture and Design Models

From Model-view-controller (MVC) to Unified Modeling Language (UML), an EA should have a detailed understanding of every available design model.

Confession 14:

> Many Enterprise Architects have one favorite architectural model they will employ regarding its efficacy in a given situation.

Architectural models are like footwear: One size doesn't fit all. Therefore, Enterprise Architects should have the depth and breadth of knowledge to suggest the best-fitting model to ensure a well-shod organization.

Hardware Platforms

From stand-alone PCs to blade arrays serving vast cloud-based server farms to liquid-nitrogen-cooled computers, every Enterprise Architect should have at least a working knowledge of all available processing platforms.

Confession 15:

Many Enterprise Architects view hardware as a necessary evil.

Incorporating specific, targeted hardware components is a fundamental design element of any Enterprise Architecture.

Networking Solutions

An Enterprise Architect should thoroughly understand networking infrastructure components and related communication technologies.

Security Technologies

Have I mentioned that, in my experience, security teams rarely ever tell you *what* to do? Instead, like Nancy Regan, their motto seems to be: "Just say no!"

Thus, the responsibility usually falls upon the Enterprise Architect (among others) to identify the components, tools, and designs that, upon completion of an audit, will inspire a Security Consultant[6] to exclaim, "Approved!" Or, more typically, to have them remain silent because they rarely go out on a limb and *certify* anything.

But maybe I've just grown overly cynical.

Confession 16:

Many Enterprise Architects do not address security concerns until late in the Software Development Lifecycle (SDLC).

---

6 Should I have used the term Security Architect?

Mitigating security flaws late in the development schedule is usually a complex and costly undertaking.

Development Methodologies

Like architectural models, a professional Enterprise Architect should be fully conversant with the organization's development methodology to address and mitigate the myriad of concerns arising during a project's lifecycle.

Programming Languages

All programming languages have their quirks. Thus, an Enterprise Architect should possess the knowledge and ability to anticipate and mitigate the clashes that inevitably occur in multi-language development environments.

Additional Skillsets

Project Management

Most IT shops employ full-time Project Managers who maintain schedules, assign and monitor tasks, and provide status to stakeholders. Nonetheless, when issues inexorably arise, the Enterprise Architect usually participates in—and often drives—the effort to develop mitigation strategies. Thus, having a working knowledge of project management skills and tools would benefit any Enterprise Architect.

Pro Tip 2:

Instead of railing about issues, Enterprise Architects should try to find technical solutions to project management challenges.

Uncovering a clever implementation strategy or finding a way to reorder feature implementation can often bail out sinking projects.

Leadership

An Enterprise Architect must inspire and encourage stakeholders and participants, especially during a project's middle phases when the finish line seems to move farther and farther away.

Commitment

Enterprise Architects should lead by example. Thus, demonstrating a personal commitment to a project's success is *de rigueur* for any dedicated EA.

Informational Triage

I've read estimates suggesting that everyone reading this book is exposed to as much information in one day as individuals living in the 1400s would experience in an entire lifetime. Regardless of that assessment's accuracy, it's fair to assume that Enterprise Architects must wade through a daily deluge of data. Thus, the ability of an EA to ignore the abundance of flotsam and jetsam and focus on the submerged treasures would benefit any project.

Mentoring

In my entire professional career, I've only worked on two projects where every contributor was a dedicated, experienced, self-motivated expert.[7] In all other cases, some team members were either utterly unqualified, learning on the job, or working above their pay grade.

That's life. Accept it.

So, instead of railing at the moon, Enterprise Architects should take the time to mentor and coach such individuals.

Confession 17:

> Many Enterprise Architects don't believe mentoring is part of their responsibilities.

---

7 Modestly speaking, of course.

I understand and appreciate the position of EAs who believe mentoring is not part of the job. Or they have more important things to do than "babysit."

I get it.

However, I also believe that "paying it forward" helps both the individual and the project.

Advocate

A professional Enterprise Architect can never lose sight of users' needs and must continually advocate on their behalf.

Communication

Enterprise Architects must be excellent communicators. Even the best designs are worthless if the EA cannot share them with stakeholders.

Confession 18:

Many Enterprise Architects are poor communicators.

Consider that on the same day (and maybe during the same meeting), Enterprise Architects can speak with executives, users, project managers, business analysts (ugh!), developers, test engineers, and so-called security experts (double ugh!). Thus, EAs need the ability to think on their feet and present information in ways that are digestible to each specific consumer.

Confession 19:

Many Enterprise Architects don't like to engage with stakeholders.

Enterprise Architects must be visible and available to all stakeholders. Ivory towers are the stuff of fantasy novels and should never exist in an EA's realm.

Confessor

I believe it's always preferable to *know* information—and the earlier, the better because when you're aware of problems, you can mitigate them.

(You can always ignore knowledge you think is irrelevant or superfluous to the project.) Consequently, I believe Enterprise Architects should invite team members to share their concerns and issues without fear of reprisal.

To make my point, consider that EAs work with numerous contributors from multiple groups across various departments that span disparate management hierarchies. (Few, if any, project team members are directly accountable to the EA.) Nonetheless, the EA needs to know what is happening quickly—preferably directly from the source. Obviously, "dropping the dime" on individuals who "cop to" mistakes will surely discourage future cooperation. (In most cases, management will eventually identify and deal with perpetually poor performers appropriately.[8])

I know that this position might cause severe horripilation on the backs of many readers' necks. However, the EA's job is to deliver professional-caliber projects, not serve as an organization's informant or disciplinarian.

But clearly, there are limits to the types of issues the EA should not disclose. Specifically, I'd describe this class of problems as "personal shortcomings." For example, *I forgot to check my code into the repository, crashed my disk drive, and lost two days' worth of work*. Or, *I didn't report all my bugs into the issue tracker because I had too many*.

Indeed, I am by no means suggesting that EAs disregard serious matters such as *I've been subject to sexual harassment*. Or, *I think I've uncovered some fraud*. Obviously, there should be no delay in bringing such issues to the attention of the appropriate authorities.

Politician

Enterprise Architects can't ignore their leadership role, nor can they actively avoid conflict.

Confession 20:

> Many Enterprise Architects simply want to tread water and float with the tide.

---

8 At least, that's the hope.

Unfortunately, that's not possible or practical. Enterprise Architects are agents of change. Thus, they must actively navigate the shark-infested waters of organizational politics and the turbulent undercurrents of reluctant users.

Accountability

After making a significant mistake, an Enterprise Architect may have a difficult day or two. However, the organization—especially the user community—might have to live with the ramifications for years, maybe decades. Thus, in addition to being "standup" individuals, I suggest that EAs participate in all User Acceptance Testing to experience firsthand the results of their—and their team's—efforts.

Confession 21:

Many Enterprise Architects have a "fire and forget" attitude.

Apocryphal anecdotes dating back to ancient Rome suggest that after an arch was complete, its engineers were required to stand under it while workers removed the construction supports. Regardless of its veracity, the story is compelling because it reminds us that we are—or should be—accountable for all our actions.

Enterprise Architects should take heed—this admonition applies to you. Every decision (or mistake) you make has ramifications. Don't eschew accountability. Instead, take responsibility for all your actions.

WHAT DO ENTERPRISE ARCHITECTS DO?

In a later chapter, we'll examine the day-to-day duties of an Enterprise Architect in detail. In this section, I'd like to provide an overview of the EA's most critical responsibilities that will serve as the foundation for all subsequent discussions.

Project Catalyst

Let's begin this discussion with another quote.

One of the great beauties of architecture is that each time it is like life starting all over again.

—Renzo Piano

There's something magical about starting a new project: We get to clean the slates and begin afresh with the knowledge that the metaphorical blank page now staring back at us is not empty. On the contrary, it's bursting with anticipation, promise, and challenge.

Confession 22:

Many Enterprise Architects have difficulty overcoming personal inertia when designing in a greenfield.

Many individuals feel intimidated when confronted with a clean, freshly primed canvas—they don't know where to start laying down brush strokes. Indeed, many folks find it easier to revise an existing image—rather than begin a new picture—because they have a place to start. Nevertheless, though apprehension and anxiety are common traits among humans in general, Enterprise Architects must find a way to push through and make that first mark.

Pro Tip 3:

Start a design with some simple components. Then, you can extend, modify, and correct that early draft as needed.

Conduct Due Diligence

Conducting due diligence is a valuable and recurring job for every Enterprise Architect. This task involves activities such as:

- Acquiring a thorough understanding of the organization's goals and objectives: What does it do? What communities/markets does it serve?
- Speaking to senior directors to understand the organization's future needs. For example, what is the vision for the enterprise in five years? Ten years?
- Meeting with project stakeholders to understand the role and structure of the IT team.
- Reading requirements—*all of them*. Would Frank Lloyd Wright design a building without thoroughly understanding *all* his client's needs?

Note that this is not the complete task list, just the minimal set required to jumpstart a project.

Pro Tip 4:

Don't assume anything; verify everything.

Act as a Promoter

After formulating an architecture, the Enterprise Architect must promote it. But, unlike papal bulls, which are implicitly uncontestable, proposed designs must undergo stakeholder review and receive their explicit blessing.

In other words, architectural designs are "sold," not "proclaimed."

This vetting process is a good idea and sound policy. Like a PhD thesis undergoing peer review, a solid design[9] must weather the whirlwinds of appraisal and criticism. If it can't withstand rigorous evaluation, it's not worthy of implementation, and the EA needs to do some more homework.

Pro Tip 5:

Like voting in many congressional districts, Enterprise Architects should request design feedback early and often.

---

9 And not just for the architecture. I believe the review process should extend to all phases of SDLC.

Yes, there will be the inevitable misunderstandings, the spiteful critiques, and the requisite *ad hominem* attacks.

So what?

In the end, the design will benefit, and therefore, so will the organization.

Listener

As a corollary to the prior section, another vital and continuing task for Enterprise Architects is *listening*. The age-old cliché stating that no one is perfect is as tired as it is true. No architecture, design, or plan is so complete, so thorough, and so on point that it couldn't benefit from some tweaking—even after approval.

Confession 23:

Not all Enterprise Architects welcome feedback.

Enterprise Architects must put their egos aside and welcome suggestions without dismissing them as "noise." Yes, the EA will waste some time repeatedly covering the same ground and frequently explaining why we "can't do it that way." However, a welcoming, open-door approach ultimately improves designs, encourages *esprit de corps*, and engenders personal investment by team members.

You can't buy that, and you can't impose it by mandate.

Let me include one tangential comment on this topic. Everyone has experienced a "eureka moment" while showering, shopping, or swimming.

Confession 24:

Ingenuity doesn't work on a clock.

We can't coerce or compel such flashes of intuition; they arrive unbidden at their own leisure. Thus, regardless of their source and when they occur, Enterprise Architects should embrace them and incorporate them appropriately.

Facilitator

As mentioned previously, in large organizations, members of multiple departments may participate in development projects. Thus, it's frequently the case that organizational hierarchy can impede team cooperation and progress.

Enterprise Architects often have the luxury and opportunity to communicate "out of band." In other words, EAs can bypass formal management chains and share concerns and issues directly with the individuals who can mitigate them.

Pro Tip 6:

Enterprise Architects should use the "back channel" judiciously but without reservation if it's available.

Fiduciary

It's human nature to make life easier. However, that doesn't always lead to the best outcome.

Regardless of comfort level, Enterprise Architects should choose the architectures and design patterns that best serve the project's needs and not lean on the crutch of the familiar.

Confession 25:

Many Enterprise Architects too often rely on "cozy solutions."

I believe that Enterprise Architects—regardless of their specific business relationship (i.e., W2/employee or 1099/consultant)—have a fiduciary obligation to the organization for whom they work that is equivalent to that of an accountant or a financial analyst. Therefore, every decision, every recommendation, and every proposal should have the organization's best interests in mind. This responsibility encompasses all aspects of the project, including architectural design choices.

The EA is responsible to all stakeholders; this includes the organization itself.

Provide Leadership

In addition to setting goals and direction, leaders must often make difficult and unpopular decisions. For example, consider that a Fleet Admiral must choose the best options for the convoy rather than an individual ship. Thus, a sleek new aircraft carrier may sail no faster than the slowest supply vessel.

Enterprise Architects face similar situations.

For example, the EA may have to dissuade an application designer from incorporating a slick new technology because of the difficulties it might impose when integrating with legacy systems.

Confession 26:

The title "Enterprise Architect" should not be conferred based on a popularity contest.

EAs must have the intestinal fortitude to make and defend difficult decisions. However, as noted above, such choices should be sound enough to withstand the tsunami of criticism that will inevitably surge their way.

Serve as Advocate

One of an Enterprise Architect's most unrecognized and undervalued responsibilities is advocating on behalf of clients and users. Many other stakeholders involved in IT projects (e.g., designers, developers, integrators, and testers) have too narrow a focus to serve in that role. The EA (among a few others) remains uniquely positioned to keep an organization's broader needs in perspective.

Confession 27:

Many Enterprise Architects don't realize (or choose to ignore the fact) that it's the users who'll bear the brunt of bad architecture.

As one moves further away from those using the system, it becomes easier to lose sight of their needs. When decisions become solely financial or technical in nature, they become much more utilitarian but far less beneficial. Unfortunately, this frequently leads to architectural compromises that have long-term, wide-ranging, and often damaging effects.

WHAT SHOULD ENTERPRISE ARCHITECTS NOT DO?

In the prior section, we reviewed many of the "dos" in the professional life of an Enterprise Architect. Below, we'll discuss some of the more significant "don'ts."

Don't Compromise Prematurely

Theoretically, architects can build anything given enough time and money. Unfortunately, however, projects with infinite resources are scarce and rarely occur in the real world. Thus, by definition, all designs—from skyscrapers to word-processing applications—are compromises. They reflect the delicate balance between a client's unlimited desires and their realistic budgets and schedules.

Confession 28:

Some Enterprise Architects compromise too early.

When you distill it, the architect's job in any field is to identify and prioritize the client's requirements and package the essential elements into a design that meets the practical considerations imposed by real-world limitations. Thus, at the beginning of every new assignment, Enterprise Architects must understand that compromise is inevitable.

The question is: When?

As a result of entering the inevitable "requirements negotiation phase" that occurs in almost every project, EAs will unavoidably be forced to impose limits on the resulting system's services. Consequently, EAs should fend off such "horse trading" as long as possible to prevent prematurely limiting a system's features. That is, compromise reduces functionality and lowers the ceiling on an application's usefulness, which is often challenging to raise once set.

Pro Tip 7:

Delay compromise as long as possible.

Don't Work in a Vacuum

In smaller shops, it's often the case that the Enterprise Architect must also serve as a contributor—usually a developer. Such a hands-on approach has its benefits, including the following:

- EAs can demonstrate practical, working knowledge of the system and its related technologies to the rest of the development team
- EAs can personally confirm that their designs are well-suited to the needs
- EAs gain immediate feedback from colleagues when things go awry

In larger shops, the role of the EA is typically a full-time position, and thus they rarely contribute to the actual development. This approach also has its advantages:

- The EA can oversee more aspects of the infrastructure
- The EA can assist in breaking up logjams
- The EA can run "interference" when the inevitable scrutiny starts to impede progress

Unfortunately, EAs can lose sight of the project's goals in both scenarios: In the former, by focusing on details; in the latter, by losing sight of them.

Thus, EAs cannot work in a vacuum regardless of the approach. They must make time to examine the picture as a whole and review the composition of its pixels.

Don't Ignore Return on Investment

Despite all the remarkable technological advances, large-scale system development remains an expensive proposition for most organizations—especially those whose primary business is not IT (e.g., insurance companies, logistics facilities, and automated manufacturers). Moreover, C-Level executives—who typically view software as a necessary evil—are taken aback when they realize the immense impact their IT departments have on their bottom line.

In my experience, much of this "sticker shock" results from ignorance. (There, I've said it!) Technology companies aside, most executives have backgrounds in finance, marketing, accounting, etc., and are thus often unaware of how enterprise systems contribute to an organization's success (or failure!). Thus, from their perspective, IT is simply a voracious beast looking to eat away at profits. (Sadly, in some shops, this is indeed the case.)

But senior executives are not entirely responsible for their ignorance. Unfortunately, Enterprise Architects must assume some culpability for this sad state of affairs.

Confession 29:

> Most Enterprise Architects don't educate senior stakeholders about the costs and benefits of IT investment.

Two of the most overlooked and powerful evaluation tools available to Enterprise Architects to address these concerns are the Return-on-Investment (ROI) Analysis and Cost–Benefit Analysis (CBA).

For readers unfamiliar with these terms, let's digress for a moment and define them.

Definition 3:

> A Return-on-Investment analysis estimates the expected profit from a specific investment.

Definition 4:

> A Cost–Benefit analysis identifies and estimates metrics associated with a given course of action.

The difference between the two types of analyses is that a CBA often includes intangible benefits such as goodwill, public relations, customer appreciation, and employee morale.

Returning to the main point, it always astounds me when so-called professionals shy away from using a valuable piece of gear hanging on their toolbelts. You know, the right tool for the job and all that. So it's no wonder that I grow frustrated whenever I discover EAs ignoring these two powerful weapons.

Confession 30:

> Many Enterprise Architects don't understand how to compute or leverage the benefits of an ROI or CBA analysis.

Say what you want about business folks, but they understand money. They know how to earn it, how to save it, and how to spend it. ROIs and CBAs demonstrate the financial benefits of IT investment in ways that C-level executives appreciate and understand.

Pro Tip 8:

> EAs should include ROI and CBA analyses as part of the business plan for any reasonably sized projects.

Don't Treat Clients Dismissively

There are two fundamental canons that all Enterprise Architects should accept and honor as universally true:

Canon 1: Clients rule because they hold the checkbook—but it doesn't always make them right.

Canon 2: Clients are not always right, but it doesn't matter because they hold the checkbook.

These two canons notwithstanding, all the following points are also valid:

- Many clients are ignorant of the technologies they are using
- Many clients will prioritize costs over most other considerations
- Most clients don't understand the CBA of intangible features such as system reliability (see the prior section)
- Most clients will have difficulty articulating their concerns

To everything stated above, I say, So what?

Confession 31:

> Many Enterprise Architects hold their clients in disdain.

Stakeholders hire EAs (and other IT professionals) because they are painfully aware of their limitations with technology. Nonetheless, this should not engender, nor does it warrant or justify an EA's contempt.

For example, most travelers don't know anything about aeronautical engineering. Yet, they willingly put their lives in the hands of those who do. So, should the professionals who design, build, and fly aircraft hold passengers in disdain?

I think not.

Many EAs seem to forget that they wouldn't have a job if the organization that employs them possessed their technological expertise. Clients call because they are in need. EAs should view this as a business opportunity, not an excuse for honing their sarcasm skills.

Don't Coerce Decisions

As noted above, many stakeholders are technologically challenged. That's why they hire and rely on Enterprise Architects—they need professional expertise.

For that reason alone—not to mention that they're the project's underwriters—stakeholders always deserve the unvarnished truth, no matter how unpleasant or distasteful. Thus, EAs should deliver unwelcome news promptly, matter-of-factly, and without jargon.

Stakeholders might not understand technology, but that doesn't mean they are mindless. Ignorance is not stupidity.

Confession 32:

> Many Enterprise Architects shade the truth in such a way as to engineer decisions.

Whenever issues arise, professional EAs should always offer *all* viable mitigation strategies—not just the one they would choose. After all, it's the stakeholder's decision, and they'll have to live with the consequences.

However, that is not to say that EAs should "dump and run," leaving stakeholders to their own devices. On the contrary, it is incumbent upon EAs to make every effort to ensure that decision-makers are well-informed.

Pro Tip 9:

> Follow the Rule of Three.[10]

When discussing issues with stakeholders, I adhere to the Rule of Three: Explain each choice three times using three different approaches. I make every effort to see the spark of comprehension glow in my client's eyes.

If, in the end, the client asks for an opinion, the EA should suggest the choice that's best for the project and the stakeholder's organization, not the one that's best for the development team. As noted earlier, please remember that, as an EA, you have a fiduciary responsibility to those you serve.[11]

Don't Evade Responsibility

We've touched on this topic previously, so I won't harp on the subject. Life happens. We all commit blunders from time to time. So, as an Enterprise Architect, don't try to hide mistakes, evade responsibility, or play the blame game. Instead, take ownership of all issues regardless of their origin.

---

10 Adapted from a writing principle.
11 At least in my opinion.

The only finger-pointing an EA should engage in is directing the team toward a solution.

Confession 33:

> Few Enterprise Architects admit to mistakes.

Don't waste time deflecting. The stakeholders will appreciate it, and you'll galvanize your team as you seek out solutions rather than scapegoats.

Don't Act Like a Demigod

Confession 34:

> Many Enterprise Architects are self-important, self-proclaimed demigods.

Sad to say, but Confession 34 is all too true. To leverage a tired cliché, many Enterprise Architects think it's "their way or the highway."

Such idiocy and arrogance are wholly unacceptable. Any EA who cannot accept criticism or welcome suggestions is undeserving of the title and should find another vocation.

A promising idea can come from every stakeholder. An idea's origin is irrelevant; the best suggestion should prevail. Thus, as already noted, professional EAs should welcome and encourage participation from every project team member.

Good ideas rule—end of story.

Don't be a Lone Wolf

Confession 35:

> Many Enterprise Architects act like "lone wolves."

Many Enterprise Architects forget that they are part of a team and cannot design, build, test, and deploy projects without the help of many other professionals. Moreover, most EAs require a senior sponsor to help achieve their goals to be effective.

Don't Be a Slacker

Confession 36:

> Not every Enterprise Architect is a dedicated, hard-working professional.

Let me address this confession sarcastically as follows:

Question:	How many Enterprise Architects work in the IT industry?
Answer:	About half.

Many EAs enjoy the benefits of the title but not the obligations. The role is more than a full-time job, and "going through the motions" is not an option.

Moreover, just because individuals assume a position with immense responsibilities doesn't guarantee their ability to "rise to the occasion" and honor the attendant commitments. Indeed, many newly promoted Enterprise Architects are surprised and overwhelmed by the responsibilities, duties, and level of dedication commensurate with the role.

ENTERPRISE ARCHITECT MISCONCEPTIONS

During my career, I've noticed many misconceptions regarding the role and responsibilities of Enterprise Architects. The following are but a few examples.

Role Definition

Confession 37:

> Many stakeholders believe an Enterprise Architect is merely a senior developer with a fancy appellation.

As noted earlier in the chapter, there is a lot of confusion surrounding titles that include the word "architect." The vagueness and overlap in definitions can cause misunderstandings among clients and stakeholders about the role of the EA.

The Peter Principle

Confession 38:

> Many organizations believe that good developers make good Enterprise Architects.

Although development expertise is a huge asset, that talent alone doesn't make an architect. As we noted earlier, the skillsets required by EAs are much broader. Thus, "promoting" programmers to the role of Enterprise Architect based on their software skills is the technological version of the Peter principle.[12]

Technological Obsolescence

Confession 39:

> Many IT professionals—especially software developers—believe that Enterprise Architects are "technical has-beens."

I must admit that I find this attitude extremely irksome.

---

12 Developed by Lawrence J. Peter, this principle suggests that individuals rise to "a level of respective incompetence."

Let me explain my issue with this issue by way of some examples. Do you think that an architect such as Frank Lloyd Wright must:

- Work as a welder or a riveter to understand how to secure steel beams or compute how much weight a joint could support?
- Must take a sabbatical from "architecting" to spend time laying foundations when new building materials enter the trade (e.g., a new type of brick)?

I think not.

The same holds with advancements in IT: Enterprise Architects don't have to "apprentice" with every new technological innovation to understand its role in architecture and design.

SUMMARY

I hope this chapter has codified the roles and responsibilities of an Enterprise Architect. Moreover, for those who have never served in this capacity, this material hopefully offered a glimpse into this profession's challenges and difficulties.

4

Decisions, Decisions, Decisions ...

Perfection is achieved, not when there is nothing more to add, but when there is nothing left to take away.

—*Antoine de Saint-Exupery*

Engineers like to solve problems. If there are no problems handily available, they will create their own problems.

—*Scott Adams*

INTRODUCTION

In the previous two chapters, we discussed Enterprise Architecture and the role of the Enterprise Architect (EA). This chapter will examine some of the more critical decisions EAs confront and how many elect to avoid them.

Let's get started.

ARCHITECTURAL DECISIONS

As noted in Chapter 2, Enterprise Architecture is about setting constraints, managing change, facilitating communication, and establishing common goals among the various teams involved in large-scale system development. We also covered the fact that there are a lot of implied decisions resulting from some initial choices, such as the selection of the architectural model.

This section highlights some significant decisions that every Enterprise Architect should address and not leave to chance.

More Than Components

Confession 1:

Many Enterprise Architects don't appreciate that Enterprise Architecture is not just about components.

What good is any architecture if it's difficult to test? How forward-looking is a design if it can't accommodate change? How robust is any development model if it allows project teams to diverge from a shared focus?

The questions appearing in the prior paragraph—among others, as we will see—are often overlooked by EAs.

But let's start with some fundamental concerns.

Component Integration

Confession 2:

Many Enterprise Architects don't formalize component integration.

Drawing "boxes" that represent components and connecting them with "lines" to indicate points of integration is, put plainly, not enough. Indeed, it's just the starting point.

Regardless of the model, a professional Enterprise Architect cannot assert that a design is "good to go" unless it contains—at a minimum—the following vetted additions:

- A suggested testing methodology that ensures end-to-end coverage (as close to 100% as possible)
- Examples of extensibility that demonstrate the system's ability to add users, integrate additional hardware, upgrade system and application software, etc.
- Twenty (or more) sample Use Cases that, when tested, would validate the design's ability to meet functional requirements
- Failure/recovery scenarios verifying that the system will meet (or exceed) the stated availability requirements[1]
- Certification by the security team confirming that the design does not contain any glaring security flaws (more on this later)

Absent the above, a pretty PowerPoint presentation with lots of fancy slide transitions is tantamount to a handwave.

Details matter.

Choices Count

Confession 3:

Many Enterprise Architects don't appreciate the significance of their decisions.

The tentacles of Enterprise Architecture stretch far and wide and often have explosive consequences. Therefore, Enterprise Architects must remain mindful that every design decision has cascading implications.

Below are some examples.

- Middle-tier design decisions may limit the choice of third-party products available for integration, thus increasing development costs
- User Interface design and technology selections might affect networking requirements and response times, placing more burden on developers

---

1 This type of analysis might include/require a mathematical proof.

- The choice of database technology affects the design of the data model, which will have enterprise-wide implications

These are just a few examples. However, I hope they convey the significance of these decisions and that EAs should only make them after careful analysis and consideration of the long-term needs of the organization to whom they serve.

Ripple Effects

Confession 4:

Many Enterprise Architects don't appreciate that their decisions not only affect system design but also impact the development environment and influence the structure of project teams.

Confession 4 is really an extension of Confession 3, underscoring that decisions extend beyond technology.

For example, the choice of an architectural model may influence the structure of the development and test teams and their required skill sets. In addition, system design may impact the production lab environment in ways that range from increased power demand to upgraded air conditioning requirements.

I should mention that the reverse is also true. That is, environmental limitations often affect design. For example, a company might not have the budget (or appetite) to expand its production environments, thus imposing design limitations that the EA must consider. Likewise, a development team might not possess the requisite experience to leverage an innovative technology, and the project's schedules cannot accommodate time for training.

Pro Tip 1:

Enterprise Architects should not limit their focus to technology.

No design exists in a vacuum. Thus, any proposed architecture should (dare I say must?) reflect all "real world" implications, and the EA should (dare I say must again?) document the rationale supporting every decision. (We'll return to this point later in the text.)

Toss Out the Blinders

Confession 5:

Many Enterprise Architects are one-trick ponies.

I'm sure most of you are aware of the old saying:

If the only tool you have is a hammer, you tend to treat everything else as if it were a nail.[2]

Unfortunately, many Enterprise Architects repeat this maxim as a mantra and, like dogs with their favorite chew toys, will not relinquish their model of choice for any reason.

For example:

- For EAs who prefer *Event-Driven Design*, all events are loosely coupled (which may lead to unanticipated consequences)
- EAs that prefer *Domain-Driven Design* (DDD) view *Entities* as the province of *Local Domains*
- A two-tier design will rule the day when Client–Server is the EA's model of choice. Period

It would be great if system design were as easy as picking your favorite design approach and running with it. But alas, one size doesn't fit all.

A professional Enterprise Architect should choose the best model to meet the requirements and not try to shoe-horn solutions into their favorite well-worn design loafers. Relying on a "crutch" is unprofessional and a disservice to the organization and all its stakeholders.

---

2 There are many variations of this adage. To the best of my knowledge, Abraham Maslow first published this version in 1966 in an article he wrote for *The Psychology of Science*.

Methodology Is Not Architecture

Speaking of "crutches."

Confession 6:

> Many Enterprise Architects rely on methodology to avoid architecture.

Developing robust, flexible, and extensible architectures is not easy; that's why there are so many books on the subject and various development methodologies at our disposal (e.g., Agile, Waterfall, DevOps, and Spiral).

However, despite their relative merits, development methodologies are no more than roadmaps guiding our travels along the meandering, potholed-rutted thoroughfares of the Software Development Lifecycle. None *guarantee* success.

Pro Tip 2:

> Using maps, methodologies, recipes, instruction booklets, rules-of-thumb, hunches, etc., guides our efforts toward a goal, but they don't preclude the need to *think*. Don't just assume that blindly following the adopted methodology will lead you to the best solution. Take time to understand the consequences of a choice before selecting it.

I'd bet some hard-earned Bitcoin that most readers of this book have been part of projects that have succeeded and failed using more than one of these methodologies. Yet, upon reflection, how many of you would laud or blame the underlying approach for the project's outcome?

Instead, I would guess that most of you would attribute a project's success or failure to a broad range of causes unrelated to the choice of the SDLC. (We will return to this discussion of why projects fail in Chapter 8.)

Planning Counts

Confession 7:

Architecture on the fly doesn't work.

There, I said it—and I expect to receive a lot of flak about voicing this opinion aloud from Agile advocates.

A few years ago, a client—an Agile proponent, of course—said regarding the start of new development projects, "As I accelerate down the runway, just tell me which direction to turn after takeoff. I'll figure everything else out during the flight."[3]

Unfortunately, this approach is rarely successful, and when it is, it's usually attributable to the quality of the team. (We'll discuss success criteria for IT projects in Chapter 8.)

The fact is every major undertaking in life requires direction. Large-scale IT development projects are not exempt from that rule. Indeed, architectural decisions position navigation beacons[4] that help project teams establish and follow flight plans. (*Hey folks, we're heading in that direction.*)

To position a *navaid* precisely requires thought and analysis. (Alas, there's that pesky *thinking* task again.) I'm sorry, but flying by the seat of one's pants might qualify as a development *approach*, but it's not a *methodology* by any stretch of the imagination.

Confession 8, in the next section, expands on this point.

The Price of Technical Debt

Confession 8:

Most Enterprise Architects—indeed most project stakeholders—don't understand the impact of Technical Debt.[5]

---

3 I need to come clean: This quote is not accurate. I altered the metaphor to protect the client's identity.

4 Also called a *waypoint*.

5 Technical Debt refers to the accumulation of design deficiencies that render code difficult to maintain and extend, usually a result of prioritizing schedules over quality.

People, in general, and Project Managers, in particular, want to feel like something's *happening—Hey, folks, things are moving!*

However, *feeling* productive is not necessarily *being* productive. That is, just because you're *moving* doesn't mean you're closer to your destination. You could be flying in circles or, worse, heading in the wrong direction.

Case in point:[6] What if you're seven sprints into your project when you suddenly discover that the slick NoSQL[7] DBMS you selected in Sprint 1 (partially because it would look *so* great on your resume) is not well suited for the types of queries your application requires?

Oops! What's an Enterprise Architect to do?

Oh, that's simple: Swap in a relational database and refactor the code.

Unfortunately, refactoring[8] is not free. In fact, it has two types of costs: direct and indirect. We measure the direct cost as the time and resources required for the development team to complete the refactoring effort. The indirect cost is more subtle to compute because it represents the business impact of new functionality the project team *could have* provided its user community instead of remediating a poor design.

Yes, I'm fully aware that time-to-market considerations often prioritize speed of delivery over product quality. And, yes, I am mindful of the fact that "life happens" and plans change. And I also know that we all make mistakes, even under the best circumstances.

Nonetheless, I contend that with some forethought and analysis, many of the types of mistakes noted above are eminently avoidable. That's why I'm a proponent of adopting a "Sprint 0," during which a small team, led by the Enterprise Architect and other senior designers, develops an architecture and a data model—at a minimum. I believe that *thought* combined with a rapid development methodology (if employed correctly—more on this later) establishes an SDLC flight plan that goes a long way to mitigating unexpected mid-project turbulence.

---

6 This is a real example. The technologies were changed to protect the incompetent.

7 NoSQL stands for "Not only SQL." It refers to databases that use non-tabular approaches to store and index data.

8 Refactoring is the process of revising the design and structure of source code without adding or modifying functionality.

Pro Tip 3:

It's better to start with a plan—even if (when!) it changes—than simply taking off and gliding with the wind.

This point leads us to the next decision: How much "architecture" is enough?

Architectural Scope

Confession 9:

Many Enterprise Architects are not savvy enough to appreciate the scope and extent of the artifacts required for a given project.

Consider two scenarios.

Scenario 1 You have an expansive backyard, extra cash, and want to build your new rescue puppy, Byte, a doghouse.

Scenario 2 You have an acre of land, beaucoup bucks, and want to construct your significant other's dream house.

When considering Scenario 1, how much effort would you expend drawing blueprints for Byte's new homestead—particularly if you're handy with carpentry tools?

Not much, I'd imagine.

For this project, the expense of "formal planning" would likely exceed the cost of mitigating any mistakes. So, instead, you might establish some overall measurements, determine a location, and then start cutting wood and hammering nails.

Now consider how you might approach Scenario 2.

Given the costs and risks involved, your first step would likely be to draw formal plans with the aid of an architect. You'd then take time to review drawings, blueprints, and mockups with all stakeholders (i.e., your significant other), revising as necessary long before hiring an excavator to dig the foundation.

Now, let's apply the same reasoning to the world of IT.

When developing a one-off web-based application to collect employee suggestions for the theme of next year's holiday party, would you require a full suite of design artifacts—use cases, data models, system integration diagrams, etc.?

No, that would be utter overkill.

On the other hand, even when employing a rapid development methodology, would you consider starting a significant project—let's say one to replace the national air traffic control system—without a fleshed-out design and without seeking comments and suggestions from all influential stakeholders?

No, that would be sheer madness.

As these examples highlight, system requirements define a project's scope and imply a construction approach. Therefore, Enterprise Architects must bear this in mind when developing project plans.

But hold on, there is one caveat.[9]

I have and will continue to argue that organizations of any reasonable size establish and maintain an Enterprise Architecture. Thus, even when developing a "doghouse," projects must align with the architecture's overarching design principles and constraints.

Otherwise, chaos will get its foot in the door.

Embrace JIT

Confession 10:

> Architects, Project Managers, and Technical Leads don't leverage Just-in-Time (JIT) development practices.

After deciding the scope of a design effort, the next decision facing Enterprise Architects is how much to build and when to build it.

---

9 Isn't there always?

When employing a rapid development methodology such as Agile, the first consideration, what to build, is typically obvious: The User Stories assigned to each Sprint dictate the list of components requiring construction.

However, there are cases where it would benefit the project to reorder User Stories to streamline development efforts. Enterprise Architects and Project Managers should be receptive to any suggestions in this regard from Application Architects and Technical Leads.

In practice, addressing the second concern—how much of each component developers should build—can be a bit more tenuous, especially for critical components.

There are two schools of thought:

> **Option 1**   Build out the component in its entirety and be done with it
>
> **Option 2**   Develop the minimal set of services necessary to satisfy the User Stories in question and leave the rest "for later"

The primary concern with Option 1 is that any time spent developing services (or parts thereof) that are not strictly necessary for the User Stories under development affects the amount of Story Points the current Sprint can deliver.[10] But, when employing Option 2, you must consider that when programmers are "elbows deep" into a development task, it's usually easier for them to complete the effort in one pass, thus reducing the overall cost of component development.

Thus, you can summarize this enigma as follows:

> You can pay now, or you can pay later—but you're going to pay.

In my experience, it usually costs more when you choose to pay later:

- More than one developer might be involved in the component's construction, thus raising the likelihood of unnecessary and unanticipated refactoring. (This is a small-scale spinoff of the "Not Invented Here" syndrome; see below.)

---

10 This is often referred to as Opportunity Loss.

- Whether it's the original programmer or a follow-on developer, you'll incur additional analysis time when that individual resumes/assumes responsibility for the component's completion/extension.

Note there are no absolutes. Each instance is *sui generis* and requires an individual due diligence effort. However, because they may have broad project implications, the decisions should be the management team's responsibility, not individual developers.

At the risk of stating the obvious, the JIT approach should extend to all aspects of a project when employing any rapid development methodology: User Stories, test scenarios, execution environments, etc.[11]

Design for Code Reuse

While deciding what to build, many Enterprise Architects overlook the benefits of acquiring and reusing existing code.

Confession 11:

Many Enterprise Architects suffer from the NIH[12] Syndrome.

I don't know why this is the case, but I've worked with many Enterprise Architects who want to build everything in-house. Whether it's ego, fear of the unknown, or just human nature, they think it anathema to reuse code from another project or, heaven forbid, integrate third-party-developed components.

Granted, there are concerns associated when acquiring outside software:

Licensing Fees At some point, third-party components price themselves out of viability, and it becomes cheaper to "roll your own." However, an EA must also consider whether the algorithm/technology under consideration is in the project team's "sweet spot." For example, the cost of a search algorithm

---

11 Indeed, this is inherent in many methodologies.
12 Not Invented Here.

might be "exorbitant." However, the organization must determine whether it has the appetite to hire or train experts to develop and maintain such a component.

Licensing Limitations — In addition to the basic fees, EAs must consider whether licensing limitations might affect how and where the organization may deploy and use the component.

Code Quality — Without expending some testing effort or conducting a code review (if the source code is available), product quality could be a roll of the dice.

Vendor Support — EAs must conduct some market research to determine vendor responsiveness. Unanswered calls during a Severity 1 outage make life uncomfortable.

Vendor Viability — Will the vendor remain a viable entity throughout the anticipated life cycle of the application that relies on its products? Again, due diligence rules the day.

Integration Efforts — Integrating third-party code into your design is not free and is often not easy. In addition, you may have to accept limitations (i.e., fewer features and constrained configurability) when incorporating externally developed solutions.

The above notwithstanding, integrating third-party and previously developed in-house components can significantly reduce the cost and time to market for most large-scale development projects when employed judiciously.

Wrap It Up

So, how do you "judiciously" integrate a third-party module into your project? Well, you treat it like a birthday present and *wrap it.*

Confession 12:

> Many IT professionals—not just Enterprise Architects—undervalue the benefits of developing *Wrapper Functions*.

Before we proceed, a definition is in order.

Definition 1:

> A *Wrapper Function* is a "thin veneer" whose only task is to invoke another function[13] after executing as little code as possible.

Wrapper functions provide many benefits at a relatively small cost. They:

- Create new or customized abstractions
- Isolate project code from potentially transient or suspect libraries
- Provide new interfaces for existing code
- Translate parameter values from "new" environments to "old"

Pro Tip 4:

> Given the extraordinary benefits at such modest costs, architects and designers should consider wrapping every external component.

Focus on Holistic Solutions

In keeping with the preceding metaphor, I'd like to *wrap* this section with a question:

How many architects does it take to change a light bulb?

No, this is not a joke. Although to be fair, I phrased it that way. Nonetheless, this question does have a serious connotation.

---

13 In this context, the term *function* serves as a "placeholder" for *subroutine, method, module,* etc.

Okay, let me rephrase the question as follows:

How many architects does it take to develop an application?

The answer is: Too many.

As mentioned in an earlier chapter, the IT industry confers the title "architect" for too many technical roles.

Confession 13:

> There is often a lack of shared focus among the disparate architectural disciplines within an organization.

Ignoring for the moment whether the individuals assuming the title "architect" are indeed qualified, there are often too many of them involved in system development. Moreover, like the medical profession, each role typically employs lenses with a specialized focus. Thus, each architect's view is very narrow, often centered on only one aspect of the overall design.

Confession 14:

> Most Enterprise Architects are unaware of the importance of adopting a *holistic* view.

The type of organizational structure implied by the above often causes conflict, chaos, and cantankerous caviling among contributors, forcing Enterprise Architects into the role of "Cat Herder."

Instead, EAs should design and manage projects holistically, vouchsafing that all "specialties" have had ample opportunity to participate while also ensuring that the resulting architecture doesn't look like a patchwork amalgamation of steampunk machinery.

HOW DO YOU JUDGE QUALITY?

An Enterprise Architecture has many drivers: Performance, Availability, Recoverability, Security, Budgets, Technological Constraints, Capacity,

Throughput, Extensibility, etc. Moreover, many of these design attributes have an inverse relationship. For example, increasing security measures might negatively affect transactional performance; increasing performance might require additional hardware, exceeding budgetary constraints.

This interdependence among design attributes places an enormous burden on all architects—not just Enterprise Architects—because it's often difficult to find the "sweet spot" among all the competing elements. Thus, in this section, I'll share some concerns regarding the difficulties in assessing the quality of a proposed architecture.

Let's begin with the following confession, a restatement of an earlier rant.

Confession 15:

You can't judge the quality of a design in a vacuum.

Consider the following examples:

- Is the US F-22 Raptor stealth fighter jet well-designed? Indeed, the aircraft flies, but it's impossible to determine whether it meets its design goals without a thorough understanding of its mission statement.
- Is a Porsche 911 better designed than a Mini Cooper? It's an unfair comparison because each vehicle addresses the needs of unique and divergent market segments.
- Is the design of the new Payroll system better than its 20-year-old predecessor? This example demonstrates another unreasonable comparison because the older system leveraged the tools and technologies available during the pendency of its development and should be judged accordingly.

What is the moral of the above examples? All designs require context if you are to conduct a fair evaluation.

However, just because an architecture meets all the functional requirements doesn't ensure quality.

Confession 16:

Many Enterprise Architects attribute too much design importance to meeting functional requirements.

What? Is this heresy?

Hold on, let me explain before you toss this book out a window and get cited for littering.

In most cases, it's relatively simple to demonstrate that a proposed design will implement the entire suite of functional requirements. For example, consider a monolithic architecture where you can point to the single "box" on the diagram and state, "This is where the processing occurs." As designs become more complex (i.e., as you add "boxes"), you have more places to point.

As we will see, the challenge is defining how discrete components can interact to complete transactions efficiently.

Confession 17:

Most Enterprise Architects give short shrift to the "ilities."

Because they often focus on functional specifications, many Enterprise Architects leave to chance attributes such as performance, availability, and reliability. Unfortunately, design shortcomings in these areas don't "present" until deep into the development cycle, when it may be costly—or impractical—to mitigate them.

Confession 18:

It's often difficult to isolate "ilities."

There is often broad overlap in the "ilities." For example, designs that thwart phishing attacks address security concerns and affect system availability and performance.

Moreover, in addition to "ilities" overlap, component size matters.

Confession 19:

Many system architects—software designers in general—create unwieldy components.

Components should be as small as possible—but no smaller.

I know the previous statement is as trite as it is subjective. Nonetheless, a sound way to validate designs is to ensure that every system component is discrete. That is, it represents a complete abstraction and doesn't include any services that are not directly related to its intended functionality.

If this is not the case, it's time to refine the design.

Confession 20:

Many architects and software designers often don't design for reusability.

Designing custom one-off components is very short-sighted. Alternatively, if the abstractions are well understood and implemented professionally, there is a high likelihood that future projects will benefit from previously developed modules.

Confession 21:

Many architects are unaware that a solid design allows for the independent development of components.

When requirements are clearly specified and designs are fundamentally sound, like the construction of the Union Pacific and Central Pacific railroads, independently developed components can "meet in the middle" (i.e., via the inter-component messaging protocol or service suite).

Confession 22:

Many Enterprise Architects don't identify critical use cases and use them to vet their designs.

One effective way to evaluate the soundness of an architectural design is by tracing execution scenarios. To that end, Enterprise Architects should identify the top 20 Use Cases and Non-functional Requirements and use them to validate designs.

Confession 23:

> If an Enterprise Architect does not feel comfortable generating estimates from a proposed architecture, the design requires additional refinement.

Enough said; I think this one is self-evident.

Confession 24:

> Many architects miss the fact that their designs contain God Objects.

If every transaction progresses through a single instance of one component, the design likely contains a God Object. A typical example of this pattern occurs when systems use a single instantiation of an object to generate unique identifiers. In such cases, processing becomes serialized, resulting in degraded performance.

This next confession is more informatory than revelatory.

Confession 25:

> Many Enterprise Architects don't realize they can become victims of their own success.

Users are drawn to well-designed systems like bees to honey. Moreover, they will use their new "toy" more frequently than you may have estimated and in ways you may not have anticipated.

Never underestimate human ingenuity.

This type of user reaction increases the system's transactional load and accelerates the demand for new features. However, this is one of the more pleasant problems confronting Enterprise Architects. It means that they—and the entire project team—have hit the mark.

HOW MUCH DOCUMENTATION AND DECISION TRACKING?

Although IT professionals despise preparing it, documentation is integral to the SDLC. This stipulation includes architecture diagrams and design artifacts—there should be no exceptions.

Why?

Well, consider the following:

- Humans can't read minds
- Teams change personnel
- Absent a formalized set of principles to guide them, developers are more than happy to "go their own way"
- People forget things like decision rationale, design constraints, and product limitations

Confession 26:

Most development teams don't adequately document designs.

I'm not suggesting you must establish and rigorously follow formal documenting practices. On the contrary, feel free to use templates, databases, spreadsheets, etc. Do whatever works to memorialize designs. Because, years down the road, you'll be grateful you undertook the effort when someone challenges you about a decision, and you can't recall the rationale.

SUMMARY

An architecture—any design, for that matter—is little more than a formalized chronicle of covenants, constraints, and compromises. The decisions leading to that end game are grist for the architect's mill. Accordingly, this chapter presented some of the critical choices confronting professional Enterprise Architects in their quest for the Holy Grail of the IT industry: The perfect design.

5

Essential Design Principles

It is not enough for code to work.

—Robert C. Martin

A common mistake that people make when trying to design something completely foolproof is to underestimate the ingenuity of complete fools.

—Douglas Adams

I have not failed. I've just found 10,000 ways that won't work.

—Thomas A. Edison

INTRODUCTION

Whether writing, drawing, painting, composing, or designing, you begin each undertaking confronted with one of the most problematic aspects of any endeavor: The dreaded blank page. Consequently, typing the first few sentences, drawing the first scattering of lines, and scoring the first handful of notes are often the most difficult. The responses to this unspoken challenge are as varied as those facing it: Fear, loathing, anxiousness, anticipation, etc.

But make no mistake. This task—beginning a project—is not simple, nor is it a universally shared talent. Indeed, it stops many folks before they start.

DOI: 10.1201/9781003414285-5

That's why I admire anyone with the skill or tenacity to attempt *anything* because no project can end until its creator overcomes this challenge.

In the world of system development, this struggle often manifests when transitioning from architecture to design. Indeed, many IT professionals don't know where or how to begin this effort.

Thus, to address this issue, this chapter will extend the ideas presented in Chapter 4 but will focus on the transition from architecture to design.

However, before we begin the rants, let's interject a quick confession.

Confession 1:

> It comes as a surprise to many software engineers that, by definition, architecture creates design problems.

In practical terms, this is the objective and deliverable of architecture: Components that require designing.

SOFTWARE DESIGN

If you performed a web search of this section's title, I think you'd be surprised and overwhelmed by the volume and variety of the results. Thus, in the absence of a singular industry-accepted definition and not wanting to be left out of the fray, I'd like to propose one.

Definition 1:

> *Software Design* is the process of mapping requirements to components and ensuring that those components collectively implement the features and functionality required to fulfill all requirements.

Although not as formal as one might encounter in a computer science textbook, this definition will suffice for our needs. However, it glosses over the fact that the word "design" is an overloaded term in IT because it refers to both internal components and the appearance of the user interface.

Architecture vs. Design

Despite the inherent ambiguity, Definition 1 serves as a perfect segue to our next confession, which we can introduce with a question:

What's the difference between architecture and design?

Confession 2:

There isn't a clear demarcation indicating where architecture ends, and design begins.

Because the boundaries are not well defined, the handoff of responsibilities between Enterprise and Application Architects can be confusing and, worse, vary from project to project within an organization.

For example, consider the following sequence of figures depicting designs of increasing detail and complexity (Figures 5.1–5.4).

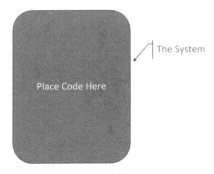

FIGURE 5.1
Monolithic Example.

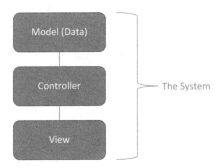

FIGURE 5.2
Simplified MVC Example

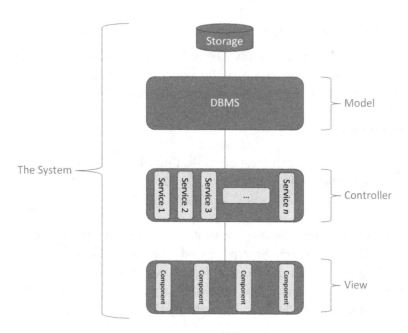

FIGURE 5.3
Simplified SOA Example

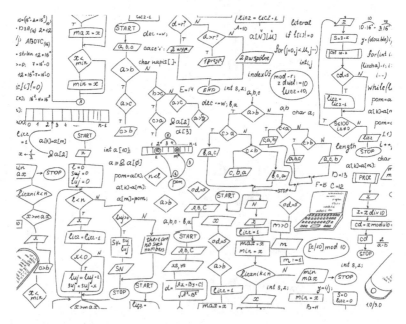

FIGURE 5.4
Complex Design Example

Although I've taken some pedagogical license with this series of figures, I nonetheless hope the point is clear. We can continually refine architecture until it represents a complete solution. And, to some extent, that is the essence of system design: A successive refinement of the architecture until we develop enough detail to build something from it.

In Chapter 2, we compared architecture to a town's zoning board and design as the plans for individual houses. Unfortunately, it's often difficult to distinguish between the two in the real world because of politics, fiefdoms, and the meddling of petty municipal administrators.

Though we lack the Napoleonic bureaucrats, the same confusion exists in IT because deciding when architecture ends and design begins can also be problematic. As noted above, the challenge is like any creative endeavor because it's difficult to know when to declare victory.

We'll return to this topic later in the chapter after introducing some additional concepts.

For now, let's return to our discussion of software design.

The Objective of Software Design

Confession 3:

> Many Enterprise Architects and Software Designers don't realize that their goal is to create a solution wherein the whole is greater than the sum of the parts.

Confession 3 might be surprising because it implies that many designers are unaware of their objectives and will, thus, by definition, fall short of the intended goals. That is, the purpose of software design is not simply to ensure requirements adherence. Instead, it's to create a new "whole" that, when viewed holistically, seems to be the "obvious" solution.

An artist friend told me that the best definition of art is as follows:

> The purposeful arrangement of individual objects to create a new whole.

I'm not an expert in that field, so I don't know whether my friend's characterization is a universally accepted definition or just one person's opinion. Nonetheless, it suggests a heuristic we can apply to system design.

Pro Tip 1:

> Incorporating and combining components in a design should be a deliberate action based on a sound rationale, adding value to the overall solution.

Like a puzzle piece, every component/element added to a design must "fill a unique void" in the overall solution. If it doesn't, there are only two choices: Change it or delete it.

This last point leads directly to one of my all-time pet peeves.

Confession 4:

> When stuck, many Enterprise Architects and System Designers simply "draw another box."

I cannot convey how much this type of professional laziness[1] rankles me. Indeed, I addressed this topic in an earlier chapter, and I can't wait to finish writing this section and move on to the next subject.

However, I do feel duty-bound to bring closure to this subject. Thus, I ask you to please consider the following:

Pro Tip 2:

> The least expensive and most reliable component is the one that is never built or deployed.

I know what you're thinking: Duh! Agreed, and well stated.

Unfortunately, architects who blithely add "boxes" to a design diagram don't consider that each such "hand wave" requires:

---

1 Is "professional laziness" an oxymoron?

- Development: Code and Unit Testing
- Testing: Functional, Integration, System, Performance
- Deployment: Create and test new scripts
- Monitoring: Additional instrumentation
- Maintenance: Potential defect remediation

If, as an architect, you suddenly realize that your design is "lacking," your first instinct should not be to "draw more boxes." Instead, you should holistically reevaluate your overall approach. A cleaner, simpler, more comprehensive solution might be waiting for you.

Okay, time to move on.

The Cost of Compromise

Although much less annoying, this next confession relates to the prior one.

Confession 5:

Many architects and designers compromise too early.

I know what you're thinking: "In a previous chapter, didn't you blather on and on about how architecture and design are nothing more than a memorialized list of compromises? So now you're telling us compromising is bad?"

No, I'm not.

I'm saying that you shouldn't compromise too early in the design phase. As soon as you do, you've established a ceiling above which your solution can never rise.

Pro Tip 3:

Designers should "shoot for the stars" before "returning to Earth."

You will often fall short of your "stretch goals." But it might surprise you how much more you'll achieve if you defer the inevitable moments of compromise.

The Cost of Inflexibility

As an Enterprise Architect, the buck often stops with you, but ideas can originate from anywhere.

Confession 6:

Many architects and designers succumb to the NIH[2] Syndrome.

An Enterprise Architect's commitment and fiduciary responsibilities are to the organization sponsoring the project. Consequently, a *professional* EA should foster an environment where the best idea prevails—regardless of its origin.

Consider the following often-cited quote:

Success has many fathers, but failure is an orphan.[3]

When a project succeeds, there's praise enough for everyone. However, when one fails, the EA usually stands alone. (Been there; done that—got the t-shirt, hat, and scars.)

So don't let your pride blind you to the point that you can't recognize that someone else's idea is better. Regardless of how you get there, your destination should always be the best solution.

COMMON ISSUES WITH THE DESIGN PROCESS

As with any human undertaking, there are as many ways to approach system design as there are system designers. There is no objective right or wrong, just results.

However, that doesn't mean designers have license to "shoot from the hip." On the contrary, many guidelines exist that can help structure the process.

---

2 Not Invented Here.

3 There are many variants of this quote. One of the earliest variations I discovered dates to Roman times. I thus found it difficult to determine the original version and attribute it to a specific individual.

The Peter Principle

Confession 7:

Many architects lack formal training in the methods, procedures, and theories of system design.

When selecting architects and designers, many organizations follow the *Peter Principle*, which is defined as follows:

Definition 2:

Individuals rise to "a level of respective incompetence."[4]

In the world of IT, that means:

- The best Developer becomes the Team Lead
- The best Team Lead becomes the Project Lead
- The best Project Lead becomes the Application Architect
- The best Application Architect becomes the Systems Architect
- The best Systems Architect becomes the Enterprise Architect

Although there is considerable overlap in the required skills, each job title in the above sequence requires unique competencies. So, what's the likelihood that one individual possesses them all?

In other words, what's the probability that your best developer will have the requisite skills and capabilities to create an Enterprise Architecture that can serve as your organization's roadmap into the future?

I'll leave that for you to ponder; I will move on.

Stepwise Refinement

The "gold standard" approach to design is still Top-down, with verification performed Bottom-up. Although it seems dated, this approach integrates well with an Agile methodology that includes a Sprint 0: Architects receive design feedback beginning with Sprint 1.

---

4 From the book entitled, *The Peter Principle*. Written by Dr. Laurence J. Peter and Raymond Hull. 1969; William Morrow and Company.

Confession 8:

Many designers ignore the benefits of Stepwise Refinement.

Let me quote you Gall's Law:

A complex system that works is invariably found to have evolved from a simple system that worked. The inverse proposition also appears to be true: A complex system designed from scratch never works and cannot be made to work. You have to start over, beginning with a working simple system.[5]

Designers should bear this in mind: Start small and evolve. Don't try to develop an Enterprise Architecture in one fell swoop. Instead, engage in a successive set of manageable refinements that inexorably lead you to a complex endgame.

Occam's Razor

Unless there's a convincing case[6] for the contrary, Occam's Razor should be a guiding principle.

Definition 3:

Entities should not be multiplied beyond necessity.[7]

Thus, when in doubt, opt for the most straightforward solution. Simpler designs have a much higher likelihood of making it to Production.

Confession 9:

Many designers are unfamiliar with the KISS[8] principle.

---

5 From John Gall's 1977 book *Systematics: How Systems Really Work and How They Fail.*
6 The case should be strong enough to withstand a critical review.
7 Despite its attribution to William of Ockham, the phrase "Occam's Razor" appeared centuries after his death in 1347.
8 Keep It Simple Stupid.

Unlike many Olympic events, designs don't garner additional points based on a "difficulty factor." Thus, Architects must remember that project stakeholders are mere mortals and, therefore, should propose designs having a high probability of success.

In the mirror of professionalism, a project's success or failure reflects on the Enterprise Architect.

Flagrant Assumptions

It's human nature to fill gaps in knowledge with assumptions. The problem with that innate trait is that many of us believe all such presuppositions are valid.

Unfortunately, that tendency seems prevalent among IT professionals.

Confession 10

Many Architects have never crossed paths with an assumption they wouldn't readily integrate into their designs.

And as an extension to Confession 10:

Confession 11:

Many Architects are not opposed to hardcoding their assumptions.

These two observations are more illustrations of professional laziness.

Unless it's patently too costly or too complicated,[9] every aspect of system design and implementation should be dynamic.

Below are some Pro Tips to achieve this.

Pro Tip 4:

All system parameters should be externalized and reside in a central store available to all system components.

---

9 Again, such decisions should withstand critical review.

Pro Tip 5:

Screens should "construct" themselves upon invocation based on the user's role.

Pro Tip 6:

The build process should generate inter-process message formats.

Pro Tip 7:

Design guidelines should eliminate (or severely restrict) the use of manifest constants in programs.

For most readers of this book, the previous suggestions are far from controversial. However, the following Pro Tip will likely spur some debate.

Pro Tip 8:

Most database attributes should be of type VARCHAR[10]—even numeric fields.

This example is another manifestation of the 80–20 rule:

For 80% of applications, 80% of their data elements are "display and store" 80% of the time. For the 20% of data elements that require processing or manipulation, programs can convert them to the appropriate data types. Modern computers have enough horsepower to perform this processing without noticeably affecting response time.

Despite the inevitable initial incredulity, I've developed scores of applications that leverage this technique. As a result, I can attest that

---

10 A VARCHAR is a variable character field.

systems designed in this manner are much easier to extend and maintain than their traditional counterparts.

However, under the heading of full disclosure, there is no "free lunch." Applications designed in this manner are often more costly and challenging to develop.

Intransigence

If initial feedback indicates insurmountable design issues, it's time to start anew. A professional Enterprise Architect should never defend a poor design.

Confession 12:

> Too many architects fall so in love with their designs that they cannot "throw in the towel" when "boxed into a corner."

If the shoe doesn't fit, don't use a shoehorn—design better footwear.

Procrastination

I've grown weary of hearing statements such as:

- We'll figure it out.
- We'll cross that bridge when we come to it.

Confession 13:

> Handwaving is the most common form of physical exercise for many architects and designers.

As I've already acknowledged, I'm fully aware that thinking is challenging and requires effort. And I also know that "kicking the can down the road" is easy—until you hit a dead-end and have nowhere to turn except back.

Addressing challenges *now* eliminates redesign and refactoring *later*.

Impatience

In contrast to procrastination, many architects want to start developing too soon.

Confession 14:

Novice architects often begin coding[11] before completing a design.

As mentioned, "jumping the gun" is a prevalent problem in nascent Agile shops. However, the reality is that once coding commences, it's become increasingly complicated to refactor designs.

Unfinished Symphonies

I want to address the following two confessions together.

Confession 15:

For many designers, instrumentation is often an afterthought.

Confession 16:

Most architects don't even consider testability.

Ample instrumentation and holistic testability are vital design attributes contributing to the immediate and long-term success of any system of any appreciable size. Such characteristics should be evident in the foundation of any professional-caliber design.

Period, full stop.

Lack of Traceability

One of the most challenging assignments for any IT shop is developing cost and schedule estimates when requirements change. Consequently,

---

11 In this case, I'm not referring to the type of *prototyping* that would aid design efforts.

it's difficult for Project Managers to make informed decisions when considering system modification and extension.

Confession 17:

> Most Project Stakeholders don't appreciate the importance of Requirements Traceability as part of the SDLC.

We can define Requirements Traceability as follows.

Definition 4:

> Traceability is the capacity to track the implications of a requirement from its formulation through its design and implementation.

Again, this is not a textbook on software architecture or the SDLC. However, traceability can address the following questions:

- What modules need altering if we change a requirement?
- What other requirements might need revision if we change one?
- What will it cost to modify a requirement?
- Why did we change that requirement last year?

In large projects, these are not trivial concerns.

Shortcutting Success

The following confession is a restatement of a previous admonition.

Confession 18:

> You never have enough time for shortcuts.

Confession 18 sounds contradictory, but it's not. Shortcuts invariably cause more problems than they solve. In my experience, projects benefit overall when you take the time and effort to complete a task correctly the first time, even when it affects budgets and schedules.

Doing it right in the short term is cheaper in the long run.

Technical Depth

As noted previously, Enterprise Architects don't need to be experts in every technology.

Confession 19:

> Designers need more technical depth than Architects.

To make this point, one only needs to consider developing a GUI or a DBMS schema. A designer requires considerable expertise in the respective technologies to complete either of these tasks.

So, does this mean Architects who have never instantiated a widget or disambiguated a deadlock are at a loss when designing for such technologies?

No.

Consider that Frank Lloyd Wright didn't have to rivet every type of steel or install the newest roofing materials before incorporating them into a project. However, it implies that he understood their essential design attributes before using them.

This same idea holds for Enterprise and System Architects. Note that this implies they have a professional obligation to remain current.

The Candy Factor

While we're on the subject of working with innovative technologies, consider the following confession.

Confession 20:

> The Resume Factor is far more prevalent than most stakeholders would believe.

Please consider the following scenarios:

1. Some individuals select tools because they are comfortable with them—the "devil they know," so to speak.

2. Others choose tools because they want to play with them—they like to "tinker."
3. Far worse are those who choose tools because they would look great on their resumes—this is Architect's Candy.

All three approaches are utterly unprofessional and are a massive disservice to stakeholders. Designers should select tools because they benefit the project, not their preferences or careers.

No Appreciation for Aesthetics

Although admittedly subjective, architects should not dismiss the importance of elegance in a technical design. On the contrary, such refinement indicates an astute, considered competence reflecting a high degree of professionalism.

Confession 21:

Architects overlook the importance of aesthetics in a design.

It's by no means definitive, but it's certainly indicative.

The End Is Never Nigh

In Irving Stone's 1961 biographical novel *The Agony and the Ecstasy*, Pope Julius II frequently asked Michelangelo (while the artist was painting Sistine Chapel's ceiling), "When will you make an end?"
Michelangelo would repeatedly respond, "When I am finished!"

Confession 22:

Most designers don't know when to stop.

Although they will never receive as much latitude as a genius such as Michelangelo would, Architects address a similar concern: When is a design complete?

The answer is deceptively straightforward: When the design can no longer benefit from simplification. Only after eliminating every unnecessary component can an Architect declare success.

Pro Tip 9:

Simplify, simplify, simplify.

However, simplification is not as easy as it sounds. It requires considerable reflection and effort.

Consider the following example. A letter written by the famous French mathematician Blaise Pascal closed with the following statement:

I have made this longer than usual because I have not had time to make it shorter.[12]

Assessing the quality of any design is often a subjective exercise. However, we can employ the following evaluation criteria (among others):

- The comprehensiveness of the abstractions
- Thoroughness of encapsulation
- The extent of information hiding
- The degree of modularization

Pebbles in the Lake

Good, bad, or indifferent designs affect more than just the development staff.

Confession 23:

Most designers don't appreciate the ramifications of their efforts.

Many architects don't realize that their efforts are not linear—there is a feedback loop.

---

12 This is an English translation from the original text written in French.

- When you change their tools, you alter how stakeholders work.
- When you alter the way they work, stakeholders want different tools.

It's a never-ending spiral. (Or, adopting an argot apropos to the subject matter of this text: An infinite loop.)

Ironically, because of the unanticipated twists and turns of human ingenuity, an application's success could also result in user frustration:

- "Why can't the new program let us do …?"
- "Why can't we combine these steps …?"
- "Why won't the system let us know when …?"

Stakeholders quickly overlook the fact that when they were using the now-retired legacy system, it's likely they wouldn't have even envisioned such features. Nonetheless, shortly after deploying the new solution, these newly conceived capabilities quickly became serious shortcomings.

I've witnessed such phenomena many times throughout my career. Indeed, the first few experiences left me at a crossroads feeling confused and angry until I understood the impetus driving the "negative feedback."

Eventually, I realized that this is often the result of a job well done.

SUMMARY

This chapter discussed some of the challenges associated with system design. We also noted how architects often fail to realize the importance and consequences of their efforts. Specifically, we highlighted how a lack of vision and forethought could lead to refactoring and failure.

6

Building Large-Scale Systems

Software is easy to make, except when you want it to do something new. And then, of course, there is a corollary: The only software that's worth making is software that does something new.

—Scott Rosenberg

Software architecture is the set of design decisions which, if made incorrectly, may cause your project to be canceled.

—Eoin Woods

The agile advice here is irresponsible, and serious software projects should ignore it. The sound practice is to start collecting requirements at the beginning, produce a provisional version prior to engaging in design, and treat the requirements as a living product that undergoes constant adaptation throughout the project.

—Bertrand Meyer

As a rule, software systems do not work well until they have been used, and have failed repeatedly, in real applications.

—Dave Parnas

Every line of code you write is for the first time.

—Charles Bowman

We have no time for shortcuts.

—Charles Bowman

DOI: 10.1201/9781003414285-6

INTRODUCTION

I know many quotations appear at the beginning of this chapter. But I have a good reason.

As reflected in these citations, standing up large-scale computer systems is not an easy task. It requires an immense amount of imagination, coordination, and determination from many stakeholders.

For readers who might not have first-hand experience working on such projects, the following comparison may help you understand the enormity of the effort.

Before writing my first book, I was a regular columnist for several magazines and trade journals. Thus, I had to conceive and compose several articles each month. So, when an opportunity arose to author a book, I thought, "No problem. It's just like writing a series of columns."

I couldn't have been more wrong.

I soon discovered that writing a book required far more effort than just writing ten or so individual chapters. It was a first-hand example of the age-old maxim: "The whole is greater than the sum of the parts." (We'll return to this point later.)

This analogy holds true when building enterprise solutions: You'd be making a critical mistake if you approached such an endeavor as the equivalent of "writing a whole bunch of individual applications." Indeed, if you were to adopt that mindset, I assure you, the resulting conflagration would be an inferno of biblical proportions.

However, before we begin the chapter in earnest, let me address the fact that I've quoted myself twice. I've repeated both above-cited maxims *ad nauseam* throughout my career (including several times earlier in this text). Indeed, many folks would testify that they are sick of hearing me regurgitate them. Nonetheless, because I couldn't recall their origin, and I always want to ascribe credit correctly and accurately, I performed the requisite due diligence and research to ascertain their provenance.

In the end, I still believe they are mine—at least in the forms presented. That said, there remains a non-zero probability that I may have acquired, adapted, or appropriated one or both from long-forgotten sources. If that's the case, I'd like to apologize to the originators for any misattribution.

TYPES OF PROJECTS

One of the most significant considerations when developing large-scale systems is the structure of the development project. In general terms, there are four types. To wit:

In-House	In-house projects that acquire and employ resources existing within the organization. Thus, all project management and staff are direct employees of the sponsoring organization.
Augmented	When required, many organizations will augment their in-house staff to obtain additional resources or acquire specific technical expertise.
T&M	The sponsoring organization delegates the entire development effort to a third-party organization that bills based on time and materials.
Fixed-Price	This is equivalent to a T&M approach, except that the parties negotiate the final price before development begins. (Fixed-price projects usually lead to interesting debates among the parties when contract or requirement changes occur.)

Yes, there are hybrids (e.g., the augmented approach could include team members who work "offshore"), but in my experience, these categories are the most common.

Each project structure is unique, boasts its relative advantages and disadvantages, and profoundly affects the Enterprise Architect's influence and approach. But many EAs don't recognize or account for their differences.

Confession 1:

Most Enterprise Architects don't consider the implications of a project's composition.

It amazes me how many Enterprise Architects assume they don't have to alter their management style or design approach, regardless of the project's underlying structure.

For example, I always design more conservatively for fixed-price contracts to minimize the confusion and finger-pointing that inevitably arises as projects conclude—someone must pay to mitigate misunderstandings. I'd rather have "the powers that be" debate the interpretation of ambiguous requirements or equivocal performance constraints rather than any vagaries embodied within the technical specifications.

This approach allows me to sleep better at night.

Confession 2:

> Many Enterprise Architects don't consider their role within the sponsoring organization.

Without question, Enterprise Architects must assume a leadership role, but their authority is not always manifest. For example, project governance is usually a given if the EA is an owner, principal, or senior employee.

However, when EAs are "hired guns" (i.e., outside consultants), their influence is much more tenuous and usually requires the explicit support and sponsorship of the organization's senior management team. Otherwise, project team members might feel emboldened to select development paths of their own choosing.

Pro Tip 1:

> Outside consultants who serve as Enterprise Architects should test the waters before making waves.

PROJECT FORMULATION

In most organizations, proposed projects must undergo a "review cycle" and receive approval before work may commence. To do this, the management team requires a description of the undertaking and an associated CBA.[1]

---

1 Cost–Benefit Analysis.

The content, format, and formality of this exercise vary by organization and sometimes by project. Typically, the rigor of the analysis is directly proportional to the cost and significance of the project. This approach is very reasonable because one can't expect managers and executives to make decisions in a vacuum.

However, the execution of this process is often flawed.

Confession 3:

Most organizations don't spend enough time gathering and organizing preliminary requirements.

It's been my experience that project sponsors become so stoked and focused on obtaining a project's approval that they often don't conduct enough due diligence to understand the true costs.

Confession 4:

In many cases, initial project estimates are so inaccurate that approvers would be better off developing their own assessments.

Some examples of estimating techniques include (in decreasing order of precision), educated guesses, scientific wild-ass guesses (SWAGs), wild-ass guesses (WAGs), hand waves, and project proposals. But regardless of their relative accuracy, when the ink dries, and the arguing subsides, all estimates are mere guesses—nothing more, nothing less.

But consider that imprecision in this context is not a shortcoming. Indeed, it's inherent in the process because it's often impractical to spend the time and resources required to develop accurate estimates. For the decisions surrounding project formulation, orders of magnitude will usually suffice.

However, there are estimates, guesses, and the fables some stakeholders use to "push through" a pet project. Sadly, I have often seen proposals that have not considered such obvious factors as:

- Contention for shared/limited organizational resources (e.g., network engineers, test labs, and deployment resources)

- Credible timetables for completing project ramp-up (e.g., establishing development and test environments, hiring personnel, and developer onboarding)
- Realistic estimates reflecting the actual costs and schedules required to code, test, and deploy systems
- Impact analyses anticipating how the new system might affect the existing infrastructure (e.g., increased operator staff, power requirements, and network component contention)

Such imprecision establishes false expectations among stakeholders. What's worse, it's a tinderbox waiting for the spark of finger-pointing when unanticipated issues eventually ignite a firestorm.

The above notwithstanding, the crux of the matter is as follows.

Confession 5:

Most organizations develop their initial project estimates without involving the Enterprise Architect and senior designers.

Presumably, the Enterprise Architect:

- Understands the infrastructure and can thus estimate the impact of the new system on the existing infrastructure
- Can assess which shared/limited resources might become bottlenecks
- Has the experience to develop cost and schedule estimates with a "reasonable" degree of accuracy
- Is better qualified to determine how long developers will need to "come up to speed"

So, why not engage the EA early on?

Confession 6:

Project sponsors want to avoid sticker shock.

If you haven't noticed, I'm pretty cynical. Thus, it shouldn't surprise you that I believe this issue falls under the following heading.

It's easier to receive forgiveness than permission.

Regardless of the inevitable—dare I say expected—budgetary overruns and schedule slips, a project with a reasonable—albeit highly inaccurate—initial sticker price is an easier "sell" than one that more accurately reflects its true costs.

Such is life in the big city. The only choice is to deal with it.

WHAT PRICE ARCHITECTURE?

In this section, I'd like to expand on a point I made in a previous chapter.

Deciding how much effort to expend on developing an initial architecture has become one of the most contentious subjects discussed in trade journals.

Let me begin by asking you to consider the following scenarios.

SCENARIO 1

You hit the lottery and decide to use some of the proceeds to build the house of your dreams. After months of searching, you locate and pur-chase the perfect wooded lot in an area with ideal weather and excellent schools. Then after additional months of agonizing due diligence, you hire the most reputable contractor you could find.

The excitement is palpable the day the construction engineer finally arrives on-site and asks you, "So, what kind of house do you want us to build?"

Would you respond by saying something like, "Start with the front door over here, the garage over there, and we'll figure out the rest as we go?"

I highly doubt it.

On the contrary, I'm sure you would have scoured scores of blueprints, discussed every possible option, and reviewed every detail before breaking ground. In short, you'd do everything humanly possible to ensure that there was nothing left to chance.

SCENARIO 2

Due to your newfound affluence, your new dream house's backyard has, over time, become littered with toys and tools: rakes, shovels, backhoes, wheelbarrows, self-driving lawnmowers with twin overhead cam engines that seat six comfortably, and the like.

Thus, you decide you need the storage shed of your dreams. And because you want to "stay real," you opt to build it yourself rather than hiring a construction firm and watching them work while you recline in a lounge chair sipping a highly rated Super Tuscan.

The excitement is palpable the day the tools and construction materials arrive, and you ask yourself, "What kind of storage shed do I want to build?"

In response, do you think, "I'll hire an architect and get detailed blueprints?"

I highly doubt it.

On the contrary, you'd probably sketch a rough diagram, make some initial sizing estimates, and then get to work—after finishing the wine.

So, what do these two scenarios have to do with system development?

The answer is weighing cost vs. risk.

In Scenario 1, the costs required to mitigate an architectural defect discovered late in the construction cycle would be prohibitively high. Thus, such risks would justify the time and effort needed to develop a detailed blueprint.

Whereas, in Scenario 2, we would not countenance the overhead required to develop detailed plans because the risks and costs associated with a "miscue" are relatively small.

What's the moral of this story?

We should therefore decide the extent of the architectural investment based on the project's scope and risks. Nonetheless, most Enterprise Architects simply—mechanically—abide by the guidelines suggested by the underlying development methodology.

Confession 7:

Most Project Managers and Enterprise Architects don't consider the project costs and risks when determining the extent of the initial architectural effort.

Note that there is no single attribute by which we assess risk. Instead, we measure it in terms of schedule adherence, budgetary overruns, client/customer/user perception, organizational politics, competitive marketplace advantage, personal reputation,[2] etc.

Confession 8:

> Enterprise Architects often manage stakeholder expectations by promoting short-term gains and avoiding any discussion of long-term disadvantages a particular design approach might impose on a project.

In my experience, "micro-mismanagement" (i.e., the deliberate ill-intentioned micromanaging of stakeholder expectations) is extremely common in Agile projects.

For example, in many shops, Product Owners and Business Analysts declare every user story in every sprint a "success" regardless of its actual outcome. However, this approach—continually adding story after story atop a fragile foundation—will eventually undermine the stability of the entire structure. (My friend and business partner, Joeseph Cerasani, coined this misguided approach as "*Fr*agile Development.")

WHAT PRICE PROCESS?

Every software methodology promises to deliver flawless solutions without so much as a glitch, hiccup, or speedbump along the way. But unfortunately, this is not the reality.

(It bears repeating that I'm not going to stray too deeply into the tutorial forest: This is a rant, and I'm on a roll.)

When you peel away all the hype and hyperbole and distill development methodologies to their essence, they all champion the following activities. (I call them the "shuns.")

Comprehension Knowledge of the problem domain. Don't be misled; this task is not as simple as it sounds. Architects and designers must possess or

---

2 For serious professionals, personal reputation counts.

	acquire a deep understanding of the world of the intended user.
Definition	Develop a clear description of the problem. There should be little allowance for wiggle room here. System specifications should unambiguously delineate the project's scope.
Construction	Build it, and they will come. Unless, of course, it's a shoddy system.
Verification	Test everything—multiple times.
Evolution	Successful products and systems don't stagnate. On the contrary, they take on a life of their own.

There is no doubt that building a system of any appreciable size requires the structure and rigor of a formal methodology that embodies the above principles. Unfortunately, in my experience, many Enterprise Architects and Project Managers (PMs) unthinkingly—and often irresponsibly— follow a process like lemmings into the sea.

Confession 9:

Methodologies are no substitute for *thinking.*

No methodology can anticipate every eventuality, and more importantly, they are not "one size fits all." Because every situation is unique, EAs and PMs should take a tip from the US Marine Corps and learn how to Improvise, Adapt, and Overcome.

Confession 10:

Methodologies don't ensure success.

Methodologies are not infallible, foolproof techniques that ensure perfect results. Far from it. Indeed, there is no guarantee that your soufflé will rise simply because you diligently followed every step in the recipe. Instead, project success requires the application of additional "shuns:" Dedication, Determination, Concentration, Perspiration, and Passion.

Confession 11:

Methodologies can get in the way of success.

Don't let strict adherence to a methodology thwart a project's success.

Pro Tip 2:

If you hit a process speed bump or determine a formalism doesn't integrate well into your organization's culture, change it, or avoid it.

To quote Thomas Edison, "There are no rules here—we're trying to accomplish something." So, take a tip from the Wizard of Menlo Park and find an adaptation that works for your team.

Confession 12:

Methodology is no substitute for talent.

Confession 13:

Talent will succeed in the absence of methodology.

Confession 12 and Confession 13 are two sides of the same coin. As with any profession, from sports to science, medicine to manufacturing, teaching to technology, talent rules the day. A skilled team will drive through any process roadblocks and navigate their way to the promised land of success in the absence of formal directions.

Pro Tip 3:

Hire the best team you can, point them in the right direction, then get out of their way.

As noted earlier, Confession 14 is one of my favorite expressions. (I know I'm bordering on harping, but this point is essential.)

Confession 14:

> You rarely have time for shortcuts.

I think we can agree that developing large-scale software systems is difficult. Indeed, if it were easy, everybody could do it. But, unfortunately, even the most talented teams, following the most rigorous designs, and working in the best environments, will encounter the unexpected.

Inevitably, when plans go awry, and schedules threaten to slip, the bean counters will make their presence known. Not coincidentally, that's often the point when Portfolio, Program, and Project Managers begin looking for ways to "make the date" and often respond with the following knee-jerk reactions:

- Testing gets eliminated
- Architecture gets debilitated
- Documentation gets prolonged
- Backlog gets accumulated
- Technical debt gets elongated
- Requirements get truncated
- Features get deprecated

What do all of these "timesavers" have in common?

They all compromise system quality.

Trust me—you never have time for shortcuts: They cause far more problems than they ostensibly resolve. Moreover, in the long run, shortcuts don't reduce the workload, they increase it.

And the reality is that, in most cases, schedules still get renegotiated, deliveries still get elongated, and users still get frustrated.

Pro Tip 4:

> When re-estimating, don't go back to the well more than once. If you need to slip your schedule by one month, ask for three (or six!). You'll

receive the same beating,[3] but you'll have gained enough "runway" to complete the project comfortably without sacrificing quality (and will have obtained enough time to let the wounds heal).

WHAT PRICE LEADERSHIP?

Typically, the amount of management oversight varies proportionally with the organization's size.[4] Nonetheless, the responsibilities of many stakeholders often overlap.

Confession 15:

> In many organizations, the demarcation of duties blurs among Portfolio, Program, and Project Managers.

A brief description of each role appears below. (Please note that, in the literature, there is some "wiggle room" in these definitions.)

Portfolio Manager	Often leveraging the benefits of an established Business Architecture (see below), Portfolio Managers oversee an organization's IT investment. They ensure that tactical initiatives align with strategic goals, develop future objectives, and manage one or more ongoing programs.
Program Manager	Based on the portfolio's objectives, a Program Manager prioritizes projects, monitors budgets, resolves resource contention among competing initiatives, and, most importantly, manages risk.

---

3 Of course, I'm speaking metaphorically.

4 That is usually the case. However, many organizations are "top-heavy" and maintain a disproportionately large management staff compared to the size of their development teams and budgets. But who am I to judge?

Project Manager	A Project Manager's responsibilities are akin to that of a Program Manager but at the project level: They plan, budget, oversee, and manage risk for individual projects.
Project Lead	A Project Lead assumes the same roles and responsibilities as a Project Manager for a subset of a project. For example, there are often Project Leads for the User Interface (UI), the controller (i.e., middle tier), the data layer, etc.

One of the foundational domains in most large organizations is Business Architecture, which we can define as follows.

Definition 1:

> Business Architecture represents holistic, multidimensional business views of capabilities, end-to-end value delivery, information, and organizational structure, and the relationships among these business views and strategies, products, policies, initiatives, and stakeholders.[5]

Unfortunately, developing a solid Business Architecture and filling the above roles are not sufficient to ensure a project's success.

Confession 16:

> Many IT development shops lack Project *Leaders*.

Regardless of size, every project needs a leader, a visionary who plants stakes in the ground, stretches goals, and sets objectives. Regrettably, I've worked on too many projects managed by committees.

Here are two quotes that, in sum, reflect my opinion of "group think."

A committee is a group that keeps minutes and loses hours.

—**Milton Berle**

---

5 The Business Architecture Guild®—2017.

If you want to kill any idea in the world, get a committee working on it.

—**Charles Kettering**

To be clear, I'm not suggesting that folks can't form teams and work together. On the contrary, I believe there's often strength in numbers.[6] Nor am I implying that only selected team members can contribute suggestions and ideas. Just the opposite: I think every team member should have a voice and not feel too intimidated to use it.

What I am stating is that, in my experience, *leaders* make projects succeed—drag them over the finish line as it were—simply by dint of their strength, personality, principles, guidance, and convictions. They champion goals and motivate team members to step outside their comfort zones and risk failure in pursuit of overarching success.

Confession 17:

> Leadership is not commonplace, not conferred by title, and doesn't come conveniently packaged as a gel in a squeeze tube positioned next to the gum, chocolate bars, and energy drinks on shelves found along the checkout aisles in supermarkets.

For many individuals, leadership is an innate trait. But for others, it can be a skill learned and earned through the experience acquired in the trenches of success and failure. Nonetheless, it is an all-to-scarce commodity that, even when present, can become squandered or overlooked by committee-constrained canons, compromises, and concessions.

Pro Tip 5:

> Let your leaders lead.

WORKING WITH STAKEHOLDERS

Despite the widespread preconceptions, the world of IT isn't populated with reclusive, introverted individuals who embrace isolation and eschew

---

6 Until you reach a point of critical mass when adding members can impede progress.

social intercourse. On the contrary, it is a people-oriented and people-driven discipline requiring extensive social interaction.

Confession 18:

> IT consulting is an excellent profession—if we could only eliminate the human element.

Because its overwhelmingly user-focused, system development faces the same challenges as any other professional discipline: Human beings.

In my experience, humans are strange creatures who are, at once:

- Creative and confounding
- Helpful and obstructive
- Decisive and vacillating
- Forthcoming and enigmatic

I could go on, but I don't want to risk boring you (assuming I haven't done so already).

Pro Tip 6:

> People skills count: Find ways to use and hone them.

Unless you're working on a one-person project intended for your individual use, every role in every software project requires human interaction. Below are a few examples.

- Developers and Testers
- Project Leads and Developers
- Projects Leads and Project Managers
- Project Managers and Portfolio Managers
- Enterprise Architects and everybody else involved with the project
- Ad infinitum—no one works in isolation.

With that in mind, you'd be surprised how far a sprinkling of kindness, a dash of humility, and a soupçon of a smile can go.

Confession 19:

Fighting with stakeholders is self-defeating—even when you're right.

No, I don't believe that "The customer is always right" or "Users know what they need." If this were true, no one would need doctors, lawyers, or horse racing tip sheets. But the fact is, sometimes we need the help of a professional to "sort things out."

Unfortunately, I've had the unpleasant task of working with a few clients[7] who were egomaniacal despots *and* clueless about the best ways to harness software for their respective organizations. As a result, they made irrational, impetuous, and shortsighted decisions based on half-truths, misconceptions, and a thorough misunderstanding of technology.

No need to sob—it's part of the job.

Unfortunately, when you argue with these types of individuals who hold the metaphorical checkbooks, you lose.

Period; full stop.

The preceding notwithstanding, your responsibility as an Enterprise Architect is to drive the very people who want to steer. Thus, as the saying goes, you must lead from behind.

So how do you do that?

By developing credible and convincing arguments that clarify, persuade, and impel prudent decisions that provide long-term benefits to the organization. (If you're like me, you can hear the echo of your parents admonishing you to "Use your words.")

I know that sounds like a platitude you could read in any number of new-age self-help manuals. So, let's find out if we can get a bit more specific.

Pro Tip 7:

When dealing with challenging personalities, make it appear that every decision is the stakeholder's idea.

Early in my career, I started teaching professional seminars and computer science courses at the university level. As is my wont, when diving into a

---

7 Thankfully, only two to be exact.

new pool of study, I researched various approaches to pedagogy. That's when I learned of the Socratic method.

Developed by the Greek philosopher Socrates, this method of instruction involves questioning. Specifically, after introducing a topic, the teacher repeatedly queries students in a manner that exposes their confusion and guides them to the right solution.

The advantages of the approach are numerous. However, for our purposes, we need only address one: The person responding to the questions arrives at the correct conclusion "on their own," resulting in a classic win-win solution.

The Socratic method is a gentle, non-threatening way for stakeholders to acquire knowledge without feeling exposed or insecure about their ignorance.

Another method the Enterprise Architect can employ is a sales technique that emphasizes benefits, not features. For example, when discussing technology among themselves, most professionals will enumerate a litany of specifications and functions provided by a tool, product, or methodology. This approach works well for those "in the know"—they readily understand the implications and consequences of every button, dial, and option.

But for lay folks, not so much.

They don't have the foundational knowledge to make the intuitive leap from option to outcome. Thus, reciting a laundry list of features quickly sounds like white noise to the uninitiated.

Pro Tip 8:

Don't sell features. Sell benefits.

Thus, regardless of how "technical" the stakeholder seems, don't fall into the trap of talking bits and bytes. Instead, when selling ideas, focus on benefits, not features.

For example, most clients:

- Lose focus during a presentation on all the options of an application server's clustering features; their concern is fault tolerance

- Scratch their heads when listening to the excruciating details involving the implementation of a sophisticated disk array; their concern is data integrity
- Roll their eyes when discussing network protocol optimizations; their concern is transmission times

Yes, there are exceptions. For example, I've worked with tech-savvy stakeholders and several former techies who switched to "the dark side" and became clients. Working with them is/was a professional joy. But they're the outliers, not the rule.

Confession 20:

One of the essential tasks of an Enterprise Architect is educating stakeholders, clients, and users.

The goal of every stakeholder is to make informed decisions. However, unless they quickly acquire a degree in computer science, most of the technical jargon will confound them. So, take the time to educate them. It's well worth the effort.

That said, remember that not every seemingly poor decision is incorrect.

Confession 21:

Not all seemingly irrational stakeholder decisions are mistakes.

There are times when senior managers can't level with you because an organization's intentions must remain proprietary. Examples include:

- Imminent mergers
- Pending staff/budget reductions
- Looming organizational restructuring

In such cases, stakeholders can't share their rationale for what might seem like shortsighted or even erroneous decisions.

Pro Tip 9:

Employ the *Rule of Three*.

When stakeholders become intransigent (for whatever reason), I believe it is incumbent upon the Enterprise Architect to show them the "Folly of Their Ways." To that end, the EA should try at least three times to change their minds. Moreover, the EA should adopt a different approach during each attempt. This bit of due diligence will allow you to sleep soundly at night.

However, if you can't convince stakeholders that their decision might lead to disaster, your only option is to build the desired solution to the best of your professional ability.

End of story.

So don't sulk, don't pout, and don't engage in passive-aggressive behaviors—it's tedious, doesn't benefit anyone, and annoys everyone.

Instead, be a pro. Suck it up, and get the job done.

Confession 22:

Most stakeholders can sniff out insincerity.

Whether a W2 employee or a 1099 gun for hire, your main task as an Enterprise Architect is to satisfy the customer/client/stakeholder/user needs—not yours. To achieve that goal, you must find the best route to drive stakeholder interests toward *their* desired destination.

Pro Tip 10:

If you want to have any clients tomorrow, take care of your customers today.

EA BEST PRACTICES

As I mentioned earlier in this chapter, regardless of how many applications you've developed, every line of code you write is for the first time. (The triteness of this maxim doesn't make it any less valid.)

For example, in my career—serving in varying capacities—I've worked on 15 or more order management systems: for brokerage houses, security exchanges, fast food franchises, warehouse outlets, etc. However, no two were identical, even for those in the same industry or vertical market. (Instead of adopting and integrating a generic third-party tool, many organizations opt to underwrite the cost of developing custom systems to distinguish themselves from, or gain an advantage over, their competitors.)

As a developer and project lead, I learned early on that I had to approach each development effort as a new, standalone solution. I extended this notion to design and architecture.

Confession 23:

Many Enterprise Architects take the easy way out and design the same systems repeatedly.

Leveraging experience is one thing; stakeholders expect this from all professionals, including Enterprise Architects. However, it's entirely another matter to repeatedly deliver the identical cookie-cutter solution simply because it's the "devil you know."

Now, before you launch your favorite email app and begin composing a nastygram, please note that I'm not advocating altering a pre-existing design simply to ensure its uniqueness. It's just that, in my experience, each organization's requirements are usually so distinctive that they demand a unique solution. Thus, in my opinion, to "shoehorn" an existing design into a new environment is tantamount to malpractice. Stakeholders pay for customized systems, not recycled solutions.

While we're strolling down the leafy tree-lined streets of nostalgia, I'd like to share another key learning I acquired early in my career. After accepting a position as an entry-level programmer and completing some requisite menial and tedious newbie-like tasks, I received my first professional coding assignment.

As you might imagine, once the excitement wore off, I became extremely anxious. I wanted—*needed*—the program to be perfect. So, before delivering it, I checked and rechecked every line of code and tested and retested every function—or so I thought.

Confession 24:

> Due to inexperience, apprehension, or fecklessness, many Enterprise
> Architects opt to deflect rather than assume responsibility for issues.

The first day of integration testing ended in dismal failure—for me, at least. Regardless of the dataset used by the test team, the system failed at the same location—every time. And what was worse, all signs pointed to *my* program.

That was impossible!

I verified and reverified everything. I knew for *certain* that it had to be someone else's bug. Thus, with the exuberance and chimera of youth, I uttered the dreaded words that echo throughout the caverns of my psyche to this day: "It can't be my program."

Pro Tip 11:

> Examine your work product first.

Of course, in a turn of events worthy of a Shakespearean tragedy, the bug was in my code. And, of course, I was suitably embarrassed. However, the lesson was as compelling as it was enduring. Denial and finger-pointing are as effortless as they are meaningless and ineffective.

So, don't be *that* person.[8]

Instead, when issues arise—as they inevitably do—be a standup individual who sets an example by reviewing your work product first. By adopting such an approach, you'll not only gain the respect of your peers but also exemplify and embody one of the most essential and elemental characteristics of leadership: Personal responsibility.

'Nuff said.

Returning to more project-related matters, it's axiomatic in most IT projects that schedules and budgets rule. And although they are as firm as they are fictional—having been developed in the vacuum of the pre-project planning phase—they, unfortunately, can't be ignored. Thus, managing to them becomes a challenging imperative for Enterprise Architects

---

8 I guess, in this case, I mean me!

Confession 25

While mired in the vortex of confusion, many Enterprise Architects miss the means of escape: Efficiency.

While schedules and budgets might be beyond our control and influence, efficiency is not. Look for opportunities to:

- Eliminate make-work
- Defer non-critical tasks
- Apply/initiate key learnings from the current sprint into the very next sprint
- Leverage economies of scale (build out infrastructure *now* to save time/money/effort *later*)

Identifying opportunities to increase efficiency is an attribute that should sit prominently in the wheelhouse of every Enterprise Architect.

Another way to achieve efficiency is through the application of technology. However, this approach should serve the project, not the development team. In other words, we shouldn't select tools simply because they're new and slick and we want to take them out for a spin. On the contrary, every third-party product we employ should have a justifiable, documented rationale, and a quantifiable ROI before integrating them into a project.

Confession 26:

Many Enterprise Architects incorporate technologies solely to fill holes in their resumes.

New is often synonymous with *cool*, but it also carries a connotation of *risk*.

So, when sailing into the choppy waters of the latest-and-greatest technology, don't lose sight of the business objectives floating on the horizon. Instead, choose tools that meet the project's needs, not just because they scratch the itch of the participant's curiosity.

The complement of aggressive technology adoption is that we can't always rely on the tried and true just because it's the tried and true. Ideas evolve, as do tools, products, and techniques.

Confession 27:

> Many Enterprise Architects expend little effort to remain current with technology.

If you don't like change, you're in the wrong business. And learning is not just something you did in college to while away the time between dorm parties and hangovers. For dedicated professionals, it's a job requirement and a lifelong commitment.

So, open a book, read a blog, download trial software, attend seminars—do whatever it takes to make yourself a force for positive change and become someone highly esteemed by peers and colleagues.

PROBLEMS WITH TEAMS

Despite the advances in Artificial Intelligence, humans still serve as the foundation of development teams.[9] Thus, the fulcrum of project leadership must maintain a delicate balance. On one side of the teetering lever rests the adage: *The whole is greater than the sum of the parts.* On the other sits the maxim: *The chain is only as strong as its weakest link.*

Confession 28:

> Most IT shops develop some degree of dysfunction.[10]

Regardless of talent, experience, and motivation, all project teams will experience some friction. And as the project pressure builds and the C-level heat intensifies, so does the trituration. No need to rail about it; it's a natural part of the human condition.

---

9 At least until the Rise of the Machines.
10 I'm sure this holds true in other industries as well.

In my career, I was part of only three teams that skirted any such issues—and two of the projects resulted in cancellation before full deployment. (Could that have had something to do with it? I don't know.) Nonetheless, working with those folks was memorable—a genuine joy and a true privilege. And sadly, like a lone adventurer mired in a hopelessly doomed Quixotic quest, I've repeatedly tried—and failed—to recapture such moments with other teams.

But I digress.

If we're resigned to the fact that we must deal with development teams staffed by *Homo sapiens*, we should know how to manage the issues that will inevitably arise.

Confession 29:

Many project teams suffer from poor leadership.

The impact of inadequate governance manifests in many ways.

- Minimal communication (see below)
- Costly mistakes that affect budgets and schedules
- Unresolved conflicts—both technical and personal
- Reduced motivation—which discourages team member contribution and creates a dearth of ideas

The above issues are especially problematic because they are often tricky or impossible to quantify.

Confession 30:

Many team leaders loathe making decisions.

Sometimes, decision avoidance is an individual's shortcoming; other times, it's cultural.

For example, many organizations discourage risk-takers: Punishment follows failure (*Hey, you made that horrible decision*), and success goes unacknowledged and unappreciated (*Hey, that was your job*). The result is that there's no incentive for low to mid-level managers to make *any* decisions—let alone risky ones.

So, what do they do?

They "kick everything upstairs." Not only is this approach inefficient, but it also causes schedule delays because senior managers become project chokepoints (in technical terms, we call this a "god object") while teams await decisions from "on high."

Confession 31:

> Many teams lack peer accountability.

Sadly, I've worked on several projects whose staff included some team members who were marking time or looking to bolt. (The reasons vary and are usually irrelevant.)

These folks avoided constructive work at all costs. Instead, they spent most of their day writing cover-your-butt emails—affecting the productivity of the few motivated team members compelled to respond to the internal spam. In addition, it also quashed motivation and created a project-wide malaise.

The upshot was that nobody cared what anyone else did. Good or bad. And the project floated along like a cork languidly bobbing in a choppy sea.

Discontented team members also affect another aspect of teamwork: Civility.

Confession 32:

> Politeness counts!

Again, sorry, not sorry.

Respect for one's peers and subordinates—indeed, basic human courteousness—should be the norm, not the exception. But unfortunately, I've seen too many strutting demagogues who seem to believe that a promotion to a leadership position absolves them from adhering to the norms of polite society. On the contrary, leaders should lead by example. And, of course, I mean projecting a *good* example.

There is another more subtle consequence of project malaise. Dysfunctional teams don't communicate.

Confession 33:

> Often, some team members lack the desire and willingness to communicate.

Stakeholders don't want to hear this, but avoidance doesn't mean the problem will magically vaporize.

At its best, human communication is rife with error and misunderstanding. Language is imprecise, linguistic faculty differs with the individual, and communication varies by country and culture. Add to that mix the challenges associated with offshoring projects, and you can easily understand how confusion and disputes arise.

In addition, many folks also forget the *50–50 rule*.

Definition 2:

> The 50/50 rule: The sender of a message—email, memo, document, or verbal communication—is as responsible for its comprehension as the intended recipient(s).

If a misunderstanding arises among communicating parties, culpability falls equally on the shoulders of all participants. Never assume your interpretation is correct. If you're confused, speak up; ask for clarification.

Confession 34:

> Some team members simply don't like one another.

To wrap up this section, let us not overlook the vagaries of human interaction. Again, I know discussing this subject is taboo, but the fact is not all team members like each other. Indeed, some individuals are actively despised. (*I know, I know. Why can't we all just get along.*)

In such cases, folks often take a minimalist approach to collaboration. But unfortunately, this tactic does not bode well for a project's success.

Sometimes, when you take a moment to reflect, you scratch your head and wonder how any work gets done and how any project ever succeeds.

PUTTING IT ALL TOGETHER

As the prior sections (and chapters) have highlighted, developing large-scale systems is not an easy task. If it were, anyone could manage it, and there wouldn't be the need for so many books written about the subject. Nonetheless, I am continually astounded by how many organizations find ways to make the task far more complicated than it must be.

If only a punch list of recommendations existed that could make the process easier.

Wait. What? That's a great idea!

The following are some Pro Tips, tenets, principles, guidelines, best practices, and just plain common-sense suggestions that can hopefully streamline future development projects.

Please note that they appear in no particular order. Nonetheless, as the project size grows, so does the importance of these recommendations.

Pro Tip 12:

Know your destination.

We've discussed this topic before, but it warrants repeating in this context.

Do you decide where you're going after backing out of your driveway? Or before getting into your car?

The fact is, you have a destination in mind before beginning your trip. Indeed, you might pause to consider the best route to follow—and even alter your course during your journey—but the endpoint isn't in question.

It's a mistake to think you can start a project with three epics, two user stories, and a promise to *work out the rest as we go along.* Thus, Enterprise Architects should insist on well-defined success criteria when beginning a new project. Then, EAs should take the time to plan the route: Demand a Sprint 0 to establish a fundamental architecture and a basic design.

Consider that development resources are finite. What percentage of them do you want to squander mitigating self-inflicted Technical Debt that you could have otherwise avoided if you just took a moment to think things through?

The correct answer is zero.

Pro Tip 13:

Assemble the best team you can.

This tip comes under the heading of common sense—but it bears repeating because of how often it's overlooked.

An old proverb declares: A convoy can only move as fast as its slowest ship. Similarly, for a project team, we can state: It's only as strong as its weakest member.

Thus, if afforded the luxury of selecting team composition, I suggest project managers and team leads take the time to choose wisely. A great team makes everyone look good.

Pro Tip 14:

Requirements Rule!

Although I believe great code has aesthetic and artistic attributes, there's little room for interpretation regarding success criteria for completed systems. Bugs aside, you either delivered what the requirements specified, or you didn't. The only way to be certain is to have a clear, unambiguous set of requirements *a priori*.

You can receive specifications at the beginning of the project, before every phase, or as part of each sprint. Regardless, don't commit to a design or any coding before receiving them. Otherwise, it's tantamount to professional suicide because when the users start complaining that the song sounds out of tune, who will face the music?

I guarantee you it won't be the business analysts, the portfolio managers, the program managers, or the project managers who usually find ways to blend in with the grumbling chorus. On the contrary, it's typically the Enterprise Architect who must stand alone, center stage, holding nothing but a baton.

Pro Tip 15:

Deliver *value* with each release.

One of the advantages of modern methodologies like Agile is that they encourage or even require frequent software releases. In some shops, this translates into weekly—even daily—deployments.

However, although it may surprise many readers, many user communities are not overly enamored with this approach. Specifically, in the little-to-no documentation era we find ourselves in, users—who might otherwise feel intimidated by automation, to begin with—can become frustrated when a new version of an application surprisingly appears on their screens that has altered or deleted some of their favorite features.

From their perspective, the system "changes the rules" soon after they learn the game.

Take the time to ensure that each release contains user-perceived value. If existing features are changed or deprecated, give users a heads-up. Furthermore, if necessary, consolidate deployments so as not to overwhelm the very individuals for whom you are directing all your efforts.

Pro Tip 16:

Enterprise Architects should design for a marathon, not a sprint.

Back in the day, there was a popular television commercial for a company that sold oil filters. Their catchphrase was, "You can pay me now, or you can pay me later."

The maxim holds for the discipline of IT design.

The easiest way to demonstrate progress after project kickoff is to build *something*. However, if you forgo the investment in up-front design and repeatedly solve issues sprint by sprint, the resulting architecture will resemble a Rube Goldberg model: Overly complex and convoluted. Ultimately, such an approach is shortsighted and eventually leads to complicated maintenance and artificially increased Technical Debt—which, I assure you, will cost more in the long run.

Again, at the risk of appearing repetitive, Enterprise Architects should take time to *think*.

This issue leads us to another critical consideration.

Confession 35:

Many Enterprise Architects don't concern themselves with long-term issues because they don't plan to be with the project long-term.

Sadly, many Enterprise Architects worry more about their next position than their current one. Because they plan to be elsewhere, they prefer slapping band-aids on issues to "get them off their plates" rather than addressing problems professionally and holistically.

Pro Tip 17:

Conduct design reviews regularly.

Public design reviews are the eyecharts that will bring into focus any near-sighted decisions.

Pro Tip 18:

Software Engineering Rules!

Although they have evolved as the IT industry has matured, software engineering principles persist because they work. Following such tried-and-true tenets results in robust, well-structured software systems. Eschew them at your own—or your stakeholder's—risk.

Yes, sometimes projects present the odd exception when practicality must prevail over principle. In such cases, ensure that your rationale is sound and that you document the exception adequately in case your decision falls under scrutiny sometime in the future.

Confession 36:

Ingenuity doesn't work on a schedule.

Creativity and inventiveness do not punch clocks. Instead, ideas arrive spontaneously: While in the shower, during the evening commute, and when reading bedtime stories to your children.

Don't fight it. Embrace it. Use your and your colleagues' sparks of genius to improve the quality of your deliverables. If possible (and practical), refactor or redesign code whenever a lightning bolt of an idea strikes.

Pro Tip 19:

Nail down the system's infrastructure.

In my experience, an application's target topology is one of the most neglected aspects of design. Systems don't run on PowerPoint slides; they need physical networks, cabling, disk drives, switches, disks, CPUs, etc.

Granted, you often can't finalize the system topology until performance testing completes. However, you should remain mindful that operations staff need time to order, install, and certify hardware components.[11] Thus, you need to factor that lead time into your schedules.

Pro Tip 20:

Instrumentation Rules!

Wait, I think I just changed my mind: Instrumentation is the most neglected aspect of system design.

When problems occur in Production (or even during system and integration testing), and there's inadequate instrumentation, bug hunting requires a shotgun rather than a sniper's rifle.

---

11 Such issues are often reduced in cloud environments.

Make sure your system is operationally sound and well-instrumented. Because when the pressure's building and senior managers are looking over your shoulder offering their "help," you never want to hear a developer utter these dreaded words when searching for the root cause of a Production outage, "There's nothing in the logs."

Pro Tip 21:

Never sacrifice quality.

Many stakeholders think that quality is free. "Hey, these are computers, right? They never fail. So why are you charging me for all this redundancy?"

Admittedly, fighting a checkbook-brandishing stakeholder is a daunting proposition. Indeed, such financial weaponry wields enough leverage to make even the hardiest of gladiators recoil. So how can a retiring, unassuming Enterprise Architect expect to stand firm?

It doesn't matter because there's no viable alternative.

As an Enterprise Architect, you have a fiduciary responsibility to protect stakeholders from themselves. It's integral to the job.

However, it's never prudent to argue or harangue. That's a recipe for rejection (and maybe dismissal).

Instead, couch your technical arguments in terms of ROI. Explain the benefits associated with a sound design. Prepare and share scenarios that clearly present the business risks of cutting corners.

Never skimp on quality. It will undoubtedly come back to haunt you like an unpaid parking ticket.

Pro Tip 22:

Set the bar high.

Like life, every design is a balancing act. Every day, every one of us asks questions of the form: How much can I get from the resources at hand?

Because of the inevitable *quid pro quo* between desire and means, many Enterprise Architects anticipate the unavoidable compromises and lower their expectations at the outset of a project. But unfortunately, this artificially sets limits on what a development team can achieve—possibly without justification.

Set the bar high and only compromise when there is no other option. I assure you, you won't regret it.

Pro Tip 23:

> Don't defer Technical Debt and bug remediation.

Because of their lack of technical expertise, this is another instance where stakeholders can often affect system quality.

With every release/sprint, project sponsors push for the inclusion of more business functionality: *We need this feature! We must have this capability!*

In and of itself, this is not an issue—it's their job.

However, it does have the unfortunate consequence of limiting the resources we can direct toward addressing any accumulating Technical Debt and unresolved defects. As we build more and more stories atop a shaky foundation, we increase the likelihood that the system will eventually collapse under the weight of its poor design.

Again, as an Enterprise Architect, you have a fiduciary responsibility to protect stakeholders from themselves. You must convince them of the folly of their ways and obtain adequate time and resources in each development cycle to repair the damage of the past.

Pro Tip 24:

> Testing Rules!

The only thing protecting you from an embarrassing production bug is testing. So, treat Test Engineers with respect. (I know, sometimes that's *complicated*.)

In addition, don't accept code that is not (or close to) 100% unit tested by your developers. As much as they don't like it, it's their job. Also, execute automated regression tests nightly and optimally upon every check-in.

The earlier you uncover issues, the easier they are to mitigate.

Pro Tip 25:

Users Rule!

We are all human. Therefore, there is always room for personal improvement. Thus, without question, we should always welcome feedback, comments, and suggestions from anyone and everyone at any time—it can only help.

Unfortunately, again because we are human, we sometimes have difficulty following through on that process. Nonetheless, Enterprise Architects should *never* fail to *listen* to users. In the end, they are the arbiters of success.

Pro Tip 26:

Documentation Rules![12]

Employees resign, win lotteries, and change careers. That's all well and good. But consider that all their institutional knowledge leaves with them—unless they've written it down.

I know documentation is costly to prepare and reduces the feature density of every release. But what are the costs associated with reverse engineering a former employee's work product—especially during a production outage?

Remember: You can pay now, or you can pay later.

Pro Tip 27:

The "ilities" can't be an afterthought

Like instrumentation, the *ilities*—availability, reliability, testability, etc.—are often an afterthought—or worse: Their omission might indicate serious incompetence.

---

12 Is it just me or are there a lot of rules in this section?

This "oversight" is arguably the most grievous and costly error any Enterprise Architect can commit. Indeed, in my opinion, it's tantamount to malpractice.

Ensure the *ilities* are an integral and testable part of any architecture you design.

SUMMARY

This chapter described issues associated with developing large-scale systems. It also reviewed the types of IT projects, their formulation, and the importance of architecture in their development.

It also addresses the implications of process (or the lack thereof), project management, and collaborating with users.

The chapter concluded by discussing some problems affecting team development and provided some best practices and Pro Tips to address them.

7

The Life and Times of an Enterprise Architect

You can mass-produce hardware, but you cannot mass-produce software; you cannot mass-produce the human mind.

—Michio Kaku

Walking on water and developing software from a specification are easy if both are frozen.

—Edward V. Berard

INTRODUCTION

In this chapter, I'd like to share a sampling of tasks confronting professional Enterprise Architects during a typical workday. But don't worry, I won't turn this into a laborious, protracted, written "documentary" that tediously shares every coffee break, timesheet entry, and watercooler joke. I'd fall asleep writing such a saga long before you would be reading it.

On the contrary, my intent is twofold.

First, readers interested in becoming an Enterprise Architect can get a feel for the profession and assess whether it's the type of career and lifestyle that would make them jump out of bed and look forward to going to work every morning. This job is not for everybody. You have to love doing it to be successful at it. (I guess you could say that for almost any profession.)

DOI: 10.1201/9781003414285-7

Second, I hope this material will provide some context and guidance for senior managers who must work with and possibly evaluate their EA's effectiveness. The progress and success of an Enterprise Architecture are not easily measured quarter by quarter. It often takes years before one can assess its worth.

THE ROLE OF AN ENTERPRISE ARCHITECT

Let's begin by formally defining the role of an Enterprise Architect.

Definition 1:

> An Enterprise Architect is responsible for planning, developing, implementing, maintaining, and protecting an organization's investment in Information Technology.

Although accurate, Definition 1 lacks specificity. In practice, Enterprise Architects must reconcile an organization's goals and objectives, schedules and budgets, and resources and capabilities to create an infrastructure sufficient to meet near-term obligations but flexible enough to pivot in response to ever-changing demands and requirements—not an easy task. In short, Enterprise Architecture is a high-level practice that weaves an organization's needs and mission with the technology available to help accomplish those goals.

ENTERPRISE ARCHITECTURE OBJECTIVES

When done right, a professional-caliber Enterprise Architecture can achieve the following:

Complexity Reduction

Quoting Occam's Razor, "Entities should not be multiplied beyond necessity." (William of Ockham, *Summa Logicae*; circa 1323.) Sound designs reduce complexity rather than compound it. As witnessed by the publication date of William's tome, this is not a new concept. Yet, despite its ancient roots, I must confess:

Confession 1:

> Complexity Reduction remains overlooked by many modern IT designers who seem compelled to include every artifice and technique they know in every architecture they develop, regardless of its benefits to the project or the organization.

Cost Reduction

Over time, the costs and schedules associated with system maintenance, modification, and extension should decrease. If not, it's likely a result of an overly complex design.

Confession 2:

> Many organizations don't track the costs and expenses associated with ongoing system maintenance. Instead, they form a "software engineering team" and squeeze as many modifications and extensions as they can into its budget.

Although this "works," it's far from optimal and conceals the hidden costs resulting from poor architectural design.

Standardization

Contrary to popular belief, standardization is not necessarily a bad thing. Its many benefits include:

- Reduces the skillsets required by the technical staff
- Developers become fungible resources
- Reduces support and licensing fees
- Enhances interoperability among components

Confession 3:

Many organizations allow individual development teams to make "one-off" decisions regarding technology and componentry.

Such an approach hinders the adoption and thwarts the benefits of developing an enterprise-wide infrastructure.

That said, I do believe that, like any other aspect of life, systems must evolve. If not, we'd still be developing systems on mainframes using punch cards. However, technology adoption should be an independent process requiring objective due diligence, informed decisions, and scheduled rollouts.

Confession 4:

Many organizations adopt a policy that allows new technology to deploy with new systems, which can often undermine the stability of the enterprise infrastructure.

This seductively simple approach can lead to insidious, incremental technological chaos if not managed closely.

Adaptability

There are exceptions to every rule and exemptions from every policy. Thus, a well-designed architecture should support rapid extension and customization. In addition, it should accommodate unavoidable "one-off" solutions that isolate them from the bulk of the infrastructure.

Now you probably want to shout, "But you stated in the previous section that "one-offs" were evil. What gives?"

The difference is in the approach.

As a rule, technology adoption should benefit the enterprise, not just individual systems. However, when a particular application requires an exemption, component integration should occur at the enterprise level to ensure general availability or explicit isolation (whichever is appropriate.)

Planning Support

Enterprise Architects constantly respond to "what if" questions such as:

- "If the XYZ contract closes, how many applications will we have to modify?"
- "If we merge with ABC, Ltd, how long will it take to integrate their systems with ours?"
- "How much will it cost to reengineer all our screens using the newly proposed UI technology?"

The difficulty in answering such questions is directly proportional to the simplicity and clarity of the Enterprise Architecture. A sound, cohesive, well-designed infrastructure will enhance rather than thwart an Enterprise Architect's efforts to develop reliable estimates.

Confession 5:

Many Enterprise Architects conceal architectural design deficiencies using a straightforward and popular estimating technique called a SWAG.[1]

Poor estimates lead to poor decision-making. As discussed in the next chapter, poor decision-making leads to canceled projects, wasted resources, and lost opportunities.

REQUIRED SKILLSETS OF AN ENTERPRISE ARCHITECT

Now that we understand their roles and objectives, let's discuss some of the unique attributes and abilities professional Enterprise Architects should bring to the table.

At a minimum, an Enterprise Architect must possess the following attributes:

---

1 Scientific Wild-Ass Guess.

- Technical competency
- Communication skills
- Leadership abilities
- Interpersonal skills
- Self-awareness
- Empathy

However, I'd like to avoid discussing such obvious characteristics as those listed above because they are, well, obvious.

Instead, I'd rather focus on a few lesser-recognized qualities I've seen displayed by Enterprise Architects I hold in high regard. Please note that they appear in no particular order, and I believe they are all equally important.

Router

Enterprise Architects serve as information routers and project clearing houses. Therefore, EAs must become aware of all decisions, directives, initiatives, regulatory shifts, etc., because such changes could affect architectural choices and system design and development. Once informed, EAs must disseminate that knowledge as appropriate.

Note that the role of router is both an active and passive activity. It's active because EA should immediately disseminate newly acquired information. It's passive in the sense that during meetings, it might become evident that some attendees are unaware of crucial information. In such cases, it is an EA's professional responsibility to clarify any confusion.

Confession 6:

Because many believe knowledge is power, information sharing occurs only begrudgingly in some organizations.

When projects succeed, all stakeholders benefit. But unfortunately, many individuals do not adhere to the aphorism that "a rising tide lifts all boats." Thus, they hold onto facts like they were the secret clues to Treasure Island.

Let me share with you a case in point.

In one of the first development shops I worked at, it was common practice *not* to share information. So, for example, when someone asked, "How do you <do something>?" the typical response was "RTFM." The nonvulgar version of this acronym loosely translates to "Read the Effin' Manual."

Nice.

Pedagogue

Enterprise Architects must be able to assimilate complex ideas, then distill and disseminate them to other team members who may have varying degrees of technical competency.

Confession 7:

Many Enterprise Architects cannot create helpful abstractions that they can employ to convey complex ideas to non-technical staff.

This shortcoming can lead to situations wherein senior managers, whose experience and skillsets are often non-technical, base decisions on an incomplete—or outright incorrect—understanding of the pertinent issues.

Visionary

One of the most critical tasks of any Enterprise Architect is leading organizations—sometimes kicking and screaming—into the future.

Most stakeholders cannot determine the best direction for their technological trajectory. If they did, they wouldn't require the services of an Enterprise Architect.

Confession 8:

Many Enterprise Architects tend to shoehorn tomorrow's problems into yesterday's solutions.

Sadly, many EAs are one-trick ponies. However, as I've stated earlier in this text, I'm not suggesting that "new" is always better. On the contrary, there's much to be said for the comfortable fit of a tried-and-true design.

Nonetheless, EAs should always consider the question: If an organization has outgrown today's solution, will a simple redesign of the current architecture serve tomorrow's challenges?

Champion

Every legend needs a hero, and every cause needs a champion. After developing a vision for the future, the EA must serve as its paladin.

Confession 9:

> Many Enterprise Architects capitulate at the first signs of resistance.

Unfortunately, concepts don't sell themselves. Ideas—even great ones—must surmount the inherent inclination of human beings to resist change.

To overcome this natural reluctance, EAs must develop compelling and unassailable arguments to win the day. If this isn't possible, the ideas might not be as strong as the EA initially thought. If that's the case, it may benefit the EA to revamp the proposal before beginning any evangelizing.

If, as an EA, you don't want to fight for your beliefs, I suggest you find a small country and install yourself as its dictator. Otherwise, roll up your sleeves and get to work.

Reluctant Advocate

Even when addressing solely technical issues, the Enterprise Architect is NOT always the (sole) decision-maker. Indeed, most of the time, EAs serve in an advisory capacity.

Confession 10:

> Many Enterprise Architects become disgruntled when decisions don't align with their recommendations.

Part of an EA's job is to accept decisions and advocate on behalf of the organization, even when the course may seem less than optimal. Everyone on the ship must row in the same direction. If the current heading doesn't float your boat, navigate a way to convince stakeholders to change course.

Pragmatist

As the ancient proverb states, "The best-laid plans oft go astray." In other words, *life happens*.

Confession 11:

Many Enterprise Architects lose their way at the first unexpected crossroads.

There's a solution to every problem. Often there are many. (Of course, some are more "palatable" than others.)

Keep in mind that, as an EA, you don't have to solve every challenge independently. So be flexible, open to suggestions, and prepared to pivot at a moment's notice.

And don't let pet peeves, petty politics, and intractable, small-minded individuals thwart your success.

Confessor

I can hear your eyes rolling—but don't scoff.

You might not believe it, but as an Enterprise Architect, you're privy to the strangest revelations. Some team members will share the most intimate aspects of their personal lives, a surprising amount of detail about their professional responsibilities, and all sorts of rumors regarding the project.

The motivations vary from "baring one's soul" to "coming clean" to "stitching up a nemesis." But, regardless of the reason, EAs should accept the information for what it is: *knowledge*. It's always better to *know* than not know—you can always ignore any "scoop" you deem irrelevant.

Confession 12:

> Deciding whether to share "back channel" information is often difficult.

I think EAs, as a matter of course, should honor every bond of trust. It's good for team morale and project success.

Occasionally, however, you do come into possession of knowledge that you simply cannot ignore because it indicates a violation of law, a significant breach of organizational policy, or offends your sensibilities as a human being.

For example, EAs should never disregard or ignore graft, theft, harassment (of any kind), sabotage, physical abuse, etc. Such offenses require the serious and immediate attention of the appropriate authorities. Don't wait; interrupt folks if needed.

However, how should an EA respond if an entry-level developer confesses to losing two hours of work after "fat-fingering" a "delete" button but is willing to work uncompensated overtime to rectify it?

I'd say the EA should discuss the matter privately with the individual, ensure the developer understands the seriousness of the issue and how to avoid it in the future, then move on to the next problem.

Moralist

Enterprise Architects should be paragons of virtue and serve as standard-bearers for their organization's ethical, moral, and fiduciary principles.

Confession 13:

> Because of the elevated ethical expectations, many Enterprise Architects believe they can't—or shouldn't—expose their mistakes.

EAs are mere human beings and are thus subject to all the associated foibles, quirks, and failings of such an earthly existence. Accepting one's shortcomings and striving to correct them is the surest way to personal growth.

Consequently, EAs should always be "standup" and never:[2]

- Dodge responsibly
- Deflect accountability
- Disaffirm fallibility

EAs should not just lead by example. Instead, they should be the example.

Strategist

There is an old saw that goes something like this:

> Although, strictly speaking, it brings you closer to the target, you can't get to the moon by climbing a tree.[3]

The responsibilities of Enterprise Architects transcend the "here and now." EAs must ensure the long-term viability of an organization's IT infrastructure and guide all change toward its strategic goals.

Confession 14:

> Many Enterprise Architects address symptoms, not causes.

You can wrap duct tape around a leaking plumbing fixture. But wouldn't it be more prudent to resolder the joint or replace the damaged pipe?

This approach should be the basis for all change: Bug remediation, requirement modification, etc. Whenever possible, dig deep and determine the root cause of every issue so you can sow a solution that will bear fruit now and in the future.

Realist

You can never get everything you want in life. However true that statement might be, you won't get anything if you don't accurately assess

---

2 This list reads like an EAs personal set of "ilities."
3 There are many variations of this adage in the literature.

issues, rigorously identify mitigation measures, and purposefully engineer change.

Confession 15:

> Many Enterprise Architects refuse to accept the practical realities of a given situation.

There is no Camelot, no perfect environment, and no utopian development organization. Thus, like a well-trained US Marine, EAs must improvise, adapt, and overcome.

To achieve this, EAs must accept that objectivity rules:

- Assess stakeholder skillsets dispassionately—titles don't guarantee proficiency
- Push aside personal issues and animosities—if someone is competent, it might be worthwhile to tolerate an abrasive personality
- Not every decision is optimal—but if you can't change it, accept it
- Work environments are not perfect—if you find yourself confronting an obstacle, rectify it or work around it

Negotiator

Sadly, as long as *Homo sapiens* exist, there will be factions, disagreements, and conflicts. Thus, any Enterprise Architect who hopes or expects to escape dealing with such issues is either miserably mistaken or tragically naïve.

Confession 16:

> Many Enterprise Architects adhere to the ultimatum, "It's either my way or the highway."

Even when permitted by organizational structure or executive edict, EAs should not adopt an autocratic attitude to architectural design. Such an approach does not engender *esprit de corps*.

Instead, EAs should encourage participation by *all* stakeholders, review and vet every idea and suggestion, then select those that are best for the project.

As an EA, you should remain acutely aware that you can win every battle and still lose the war. If you don't believe that's possible, I encourage you to read a book describing the military and political history of the US government's involvement in the Viet Nam war.

A DAY IN THE LIFE

Now that we understand the required skill sets, let's see how Enterprise Architects put them to use during a typical workday.

Before we begin, however, I'd like to share one caveat.

Every individual is unique, every project is different, and every organization is distinctive. Thus, I can only speak for myself and a handful of other EAs I've worked with regarding the trials and tribulations of a typical workday. Consequently, some EAs might not relate—or may even take exception—to some (or all of) the following material. So let me apologize in advance and say that, in my defense, this section only reflects my experiences.

Okay, enough equivocation; let's get to it.

Typical Day

I've always been a "morning person," so I usually begin my day before the sun peeks over the horizon. However, my early start is not just a consequence of my circadian rhythms. On the contrary, I believe it's essential that Enterprise Architects jump-start their workday.

Generally speaking, an EA's duties span two main categories: Their own responsibilities and assisting all other project team members with theirs. Thus, I prefer to complete my work as early as possible, allowing me the flexibility to spend the rest of my day helping others and, of course, responding to surprises.

Confession 17:

Many stakeholders use email to "paint" a "customized" record of "reality."

After acquiring and consuming the requisite amount of caffeine, I begin each day by "working" my emails. The "public" reason is that I want to always remain current with issues. The private reason is that many stakeholders weaponize this communication medium. Thus, if you don't monitor your inbox diligently, you may spend too much time "correcting the record" rather than addressing genuine project concerns. It's a supreme waste of time, but unfortunately, there's no avoiding it.

The next task on my list is meeting preparation. Specifically, I review my calendar and prepare notes, materials, and questions for the actual, anticipated, or hidden agendas.

Confession 18:

Meetings are a necessary evil.

You can kick and moan and pound your fists on your desk, but meetings are a way of life for Enterprise Architects. Deal with it.

Meeting agendas are as varied as the stakeholders in attendance:

- Team Leads—Technical issues
- Architects—Design concerns
- Developers—Algorithm reviews
- Portfolio Managers—Aligning business needs with project scope definitions
- Program Managers—Resource contention across projects
- Project Managers—Schedule revision implications
- Business Analysts—Requirement changes
- Senior Executives—Demanding clarity on why the project is late and over budget
- Network Engineers—Bandwidth issues
- Database Administrators—Data integrity concerns
- Test Engineers—Clarity on performance test scenarios
- Operations Staff—Hardware configuration issues
- Security Analysts—Results of the most recent penetration test
- Users—User Interface shortcomings

This list is but a smattering. Nonetheless, as an EA, you must ensure you're armed well enough to meet every meeting's onslaught.

Confession 19:

Many Enterprise Architects suffer from "cubism."

Please note that the "cubism" reference in Confession 19 does not refer to the painting style pioneered by Pablo Picasso and Georges Braque. Instead, it alludes to Enterprise Architects who spend most of their time sequestered in their cubicles issuing tome-like emails. Like an unmotivated salesperson, EAs who spend too much time at their desks are not doing their jobs.

When projects run "hot," I typically average five to six hours of meetings each day. I know that number seems shockingly high but remember that one of an EA's primary responsibilities is knowledge acquisition and dissemination. Meetings are a (reasonably efficient) way to achieve that goal.

Unfortunately, I don't have much helpful, actionable advice regarding making meetings more efficient. The only tips I can provide are to keep them short and meet with all stakeholder groups as often as is practical.

Confession 20:

Enterprise architects do most of their work in "real-time."

An Enterprise Architect's day often includes responding to and resolving various issues "in the moment." Thus, EAs must feel confident enough to make decisions with little time for contemplation and reflection.

This job requirement is not easy for many EAs to fulfill. The pressure is often enormous, and a mistake could have disastrous consequences for the project. Moreover, many EAs fail to recognize it's not only the "big" decisions that have an enormous impact. Many "throw-away" or implied conclusions are just as important.

For example:

- Should we integrate the new shareware library to implement <insert function of choice> or roll our own?
- The user stories for <insert the sprint of your choice> are still in flux; should we begin implementation?

- We keep getting the <insert the warning diagnostic message of choice> from the new UI package; should we investigate it?
- The design of <insert the name of the application of choice> fails to adhere to the organization's design principles; should we deploy it?

One could say that the life of an Enterprise Architect is like that of an action movie hero (sadly, sans the fame and fortune): A series of mundane moments punctuated by periods of punishing pressure.

Many EAs move on to other vocations because of the real-time demands of the profession, but it's nothing anyone should be embarrassed about, nor is it a shortcoming, *per se*. It's no different than any other attribute; some folks are proficient at it, and others are not.

Typical Tasks

Again, avoiding the minutiae, some of the most common duties performed by Enterprise Architects are as follows.

- Redesign architectures, systems, and applications because of a change in organizational direction, an unexpected technical challenge, or a late-breaking change in requirements.
- Review application designs proposed by development teams to ensure architectural conformity, requirements adherence (especially the non-functional "ilities"), and technological compliance.
- Direct colleagues to the appropriate resources to address and resolve problems and issues.
- Explain technology formally and informally, depending on the stakeholder's needs.
- Interview candidates.
- Resolve disputes. The most common are requirements interpretation, design options, and component selection.
- Demystify the interdependent relationship among the four fundamental attributes of a project: cost, performance, functionality, and schedule. They are elements inextricably intertwined to the bewilderment of many stakeholders.
- Explain the meaning and relative benefits of the "ilities"—especially the difference between *availability* and *reliability*. Unfortunately, the distinction between those two attributes seems challenging for some stakeholders (both technical and non-technical) to reconcile.

- Review/evaluate new technologies for immediate and future adoption. This task implies that all EAs should spend a significant portion (~20%) of their time remaining current (see Pro Tip 19). Please note that EAs who work as consultants (i.e., 1099 employees) will likely have to undertake this task on their own time and dime.

Some less common tasks include:

- Help develop and review a Capability Model[4] for your organization
- Review the IT infrastructure/capabilities of a potential merger candidate
- Prepare an overview of your organization's IT infrastructure/ capabilities for review by a potential suitor
- Prepare and present a spending justification to senior executives and board members
- Attend trade shows
- Deliver talks to a variety of audiences

ADDITIONAL CHALLENGES

In the prior sections, we presented many challenges Enterprise Architects must confront. In this section, there are a few—somewhat more sensitive— burdens I'd like to address.

Problem Analysis

Regardless of their type, when problems arise, it often becomes the responsibility of the Enterprise Architect to determine their root cause and develop appropriate resolutions or mitigation strategies. As might seem obvious, the EA requires an accurate assessment of the situation— i.e., the *truth*—to accomplish this task.

Unfortunately, truth is among the rarest of commodities. Indeed, Gustave Flaubert famously stated that "There is no truth. There is only perception."

---

4 This is a crucial component of a Business Architecture.

I prefer the way the character Dr. Gregory House repeatedly expresses this same idea on the television show *House* "Everybody Lies." However, I want to extend his comment to include the phrase, "Everybody points fingers."

When issues arise and jobs are on the line, folks are afraid and embarrassed and sometimes discover their actions could be deemed incompetent. Thus, in response, it's unsurprising that many individuals transition to defense mode: They deny, deflect, and derail.

Unfortunately, it's often incumbent upon the EA to wade through the flotsam and jetsam resulting from the "not me syndrome" to discover the fountainhead of the obfuscation.

But take heart, to quote *House* again, "Truth begins in lies."

Fiduciary Responsibility

It might not state so on your resume or appear as a highlighted bullet item on your job requirements, but an Enterprise Architect's primary responsibility is one of a Fiduciary: Every day, EAs must preserve and protect their organization's IT investment.

EAs can find this obligation demanding for many reasons, not the least of which is the love of *technology*. That's why we took the position in the first place: The thrill and challenge required to turn blank sheets of paper into *solutions*.

I mean, who really wants to deal with issues like capital expenditures, return on investment, depreciation, etc.? That's for the "bean counters" in the finance department. After all, we're technologists, not accountants.

Alas, if only that were the case.

But, unfortunately, it's not. Every decision you make as an EA has financial implications:

- The revised design of the <insert name here> subsystem will cost time and money and might impact your organization's tax filing regarding capital investment
- Moving the <insert name here> application to "the cloud" might reduce operational costs, but it will also likely affect the company's balance sheet, converting capital investment into cash expenses

- Deciding to forego the final round of testing might save time and money, but it could also negatively affect customer expectations and future revenue

As distasteful as it might seem to some, a professional Enterprise Architect must consider such concerns with every decision.

Walking Target

Have you ever felt like you had a bullseye painted on your back? Or that the fleeting dot of red light you saw flash across your chest originated from a laser scope? Or that everyone in a conference room was talking about you because they all stopped speaking as soon as you entered?

If you have, you've likely worked as a hired gun—and by that, I mean an outside consultant.

Because of their narrow viewpoints, employees are often ill-equipped to appreciate organizational concerns beyond their limited perspectives. As a result, C-level executives often employ external consultants to help broaden perceptions.

Frequently, this solution is less than appreciated by impacted stakeholders because no one likes outsiders:

- They don't know how we do things
- They don't know our systems
- They don't understand our industry
- Management should've put <so and so> in charge of the project

Consultants should not take these responses personally. Again, it's simply a matter of human nature. Nonetheless, it rarely occurs to those individuals griping about the interloper that senior management didn't opt for this course of action simply due to boredom or some imprudent compulsion to spend beaucoup bucks. Rightly or wrongly, the executives are trying to address a (real or perceived) problem.

So how should the in-house team deal with the outsider?

The best approach for employees is to help solve the problem as quickly as possible, rendering the intruder nothing but a memory.

Do the employees consider that? Usually, the answer is no.

While working with an outside consultant, employees can acquire knowledge, new skills, and fresh viewpoints.

Do the employees consider that? Usually, the answer is no.

If the project fails, the consultant is a built-in scapegoat.

Do the employees consider that? Usually, the answer is no.

If you're a "hired gun," you should expect that full-time employees will likely resent your participation, especially if your decisions hold sway over them. Thus, as an "outsider," expect to have:

- Pertinent knowledge withheld from you
- Every decision second-guessed
- Most recommendations ignored
- Your authority challenged

Again, no reason to gripe; that's life as a consultant.

Just remember that if the job of an EA were simple, everyone could do it.

PRO TIPS

The German philosopher Friedrich Nietzsche famously observed, "That which does not kill us makes us stronger." Such an ideology takes much of the sting out of our failures and misfortunes.

But what of our successes? Who doesn't like a pat on the back now and then?

Throughout my career, I've discovered that most people are quick to gripe but slow to praise. Thus, I've come to realize that accolades are indeed precious.

But surprisingly, I've also grudgingly learned that the scars of failure are much more valuable. Each wound records a lesson, and every lesion becomes a permanent reminder.

People, technology, and even morals change. Experience, however, is permanent. Below are some tips and suggestions earned and learned the old-fashioned way.

Readers should not ascribe any significance to the order of their presentation.

Pro Tip 1:

Be responsive.

Don't ignore emails, dodge phone calls, or let voicemails go unanswered. Problems don't solve themselves. Thus, Enterprise Architects who consider themselves *professional* must remain approachable and responsive, addressing issues directly and promptly.

The above notwithstanding, it is certainly appropriate to triage concerns. For example, you might consider delaying a discussion of UI color options to address a possible architectural shortcoming uncovered by the security team.

Nonetheless, EAs should acknowledge the UI concern and inform affected stakeholders that their issue is "in the queue." No one likes to feel ignored; every problem is important to someone.

Pro Tip 2:

Don't engage in handwaves.

Every change has ripple effects. So, for example, if stakeholders are considering a new initiative or a shift in project focus, professional Enterprise Architects should take the appropriate time and effort to understand the issues and implications before issuing an opinion.

Pro Tip 3:

Provide realistic schedules.

Always provide candid, considered assessments even when anticipating stakeholder pushback. Offering overly optimistic estimates (i.e., lying) might spare the EA some short-term grief, but one may kick the can down the road only so far.

As I mentioned earlier, my estimation algorithm is as follows:

PUBLISHED ESTIMATE = MY BEST ESTIMATE × 2 × 1.20

In English, this expression reads as follows:

Take your best estimate, double it, then add a 20% cushion.

You might scoff, but this little formula has served me well throughout my career. And to forestall the anticipated avalanche of nastygrams, it's not "lying." On the contrary, this little equation accounts for the unaccountable.

Remember that, regardless of your estimating approach, you'll never be correct 100% of the time. Moreover, it's a lose–lose proposition. Unless you hit the date exactly, you're either a lousy estimator or a poor project manager.

What can I say? Shrug your shoulders and accept that that's life in the digital jungle.

Pro Tip 4:

If the schedule slips, wear it.

Pro Tip 4 serves as a corollary to Pro Tip 3.

Life happens. Don't deflect, point fingers, or claim ignorance when schedules or budgets go awry. Instead, own up to the issue and work hard to mitigate it.

Pro Tip 5:

Ask for more time than you need.

Pro Tip 5 is a natural extension of Pro Tip 4.

Anyone who has had to go hat-in-hand to stakeholders and ask for more time or money knows how unpleasant that task is. You quickly learn that you don't want to experience this predicament more than once.

Thus, when you must "face the music," why not turn up the volume? Ask for more time than you think you'll need. Let me assure you, the pain you'll endure is the same whether you ask for two months or three.

So, go big or go home.

Pro Tip 6:

Delay significant decisions for as long as you can.

Let me state up front that this approach is not procrastination. Consider that, every day, the world changes, you grow wiser, and new ideas emerge from all quarters. Thus, it benefits you to wait as long as possible before pulling the trigger on significant decisions.

Leveraging the extra time can only work in your favor.

Pro Tip 7:

Own up to your mistakes.

No one is perfect, including Enterprise Architects. Nonetheless, stakeholders must trust their EAs and rely on their opinions, observations, and recommendations.

Therefore, be stand up and own up.

You'll gain immeasurable respect from colleagues and the enduring confidence of stakeholders—at least until the next issue arises. Sadly, in many shops, you're only as good as your most recent decision.

In addition, refrain from throwing other team members "under the bus." It's unprofessional, unbecoming, and, from a practical perspective, lacks any upside. Remember, you're the driver and ultimately responsible for everything during the project's journey.

Pro Tip 8:

> Explicitly determine during the early stages of a project which of the four fundamental project attributes—cost, performance, functionality, and schedule—are most important to your stakeholders.

Don't assume—ask. Better yet, verify frequently. Then, when the inevitable complications arise, develop mitigation strategies that align with the stakeholders' priorities, not yours.

Always remember that regardless of your employment status—W2 or 1099—you're the hired help.

Pro Tip 9:

> Track backlog and technical debt closely because they are early warning indicators of widespread project issues.

Backlog and technical debt develop for numerous causes, including:

- Underperforming development teams
- Fundamental architectural issues
- Application design shortcomings
- Poor project management
- Requirements confusion
- Feature creep

As the above list notes, these registers expand for a *reason*. So don't just triage them for the next sprint to appease users and placate project managers. Instead, analyze them to uncover the root causes (which may be many) and address the underlying issues systematically.

It's a constant battle: On one side, Business Analysts want to add more features. On the other, development teams want to ensure the system won't collapse under its own weight. (We'll return to this subject in the next chapter when we review why projects fail.)

Learn to use backlog and technical debt as weapons to fight for resources.

Pro Tip 10:

Always remain professional.

Be self-effacing. Whenever you prevail, don't gloat. Instead, reach out to those who might feel slighted and find ways to get them vested in your solution.

Alternatively, don't be petty or petulant when your arguments fall short, or your proposals fail to persuade. Instead, throw your efforts into the approved solutions as if they were your own.

Pro Tip 11:

Address bugs as they arise.

To paraphrase the oft-rumored approach to voting in Chicago: Fix bugs early and often. Otherwise, they will compound and undermine your architectural foundation.

This is one of the rare cases when fighting with stakeholders is appropriate because they often lack an appreciation of how costly bugs are to rectify late in the development cycle—or worse, after the product has already been deployed to Production.

Pro Tip 12:

Never forget that politics rule.

Despite personal expectations or professional aspirations, Enterprise Architects are not just technicians or computer scientists. Instead, EAs must become part-time politicians because, like it or not, organizational politics rule.

As an EA, you need to consider your options. For example, you could hold fast to your convictions allowing what you believe to be the perfect system to die on the vine. Or, through negotiation, you could stand up an excellent compromise, allowing it to take root and flower.

It's your call.

Pro Tip 13:

> Verify everything—personally.

In most shops, everything that occurs—good and bad—falls under the purview of the Enterprise Architect. Still, the EA can't possibly "do it all" for fear of becoming a bottleneck.

As a result, EAs should—and must—delegate.

Nonetheless, EAs can't sit back with their feet up on their desks, expecting (hoping for) a great outcome. Thus, EAs should validate, review, and spot-check *everything*:

- Designs—many will miss the mark on the "ilities"
- Schedules—these serve as a wellspring of creative fiction
- Progress estimates—developers have imaginative interpretations they are more than happy to share
- Code—EAs are often surprised at what they find *missing*
- Test scripts—EAs are frequently shocked at the unverified functionality they uncover
- Unit test coverage—even the best developers get lazy with this task
- Requirements analysis—EAs need to be diligent in ensuring traceability
- Et al

EAs that give short shrift to this responsibility do so at their own risk.

Please note, however, that there is a fine line between diligence and obsession. Thus, EAs must resist the temptation to become "control freaks." A "heavy hand" will often cause significant adverse ripple effects to propagate throughout the project.

This path is often challenging for the EA to navigate. However, please remember that when the metaphorical fecal matter meets the figurative fan, it's the EA that will need to shower.

Pro Tip 14:

> Project sponsors who manage the IT budgets hold more power than you might otherwise imagine.

Checkbook-wielding stakeholders might not always be right, but they are never wrong.

Deal with it.

Pro Tip 15:

Do your homework.

Pro Tip 16:

Don't rely on Project Managers.

I'll address Pro Tip 15 and Pro Tip 16 together.

Successful Enterprise Architects are not just technologists. They must understand their organization's *business*: Its goals, markets, assets, structure, how it functions, etc. Incorporating such knowledge is integral to developing an adaptable architecture that can withstand the test of time.

EAs must also remain objective about their organization's missing assets. Are there fissures in the infrastructure? Do we need additional staff to address cracks in the schedule? Do you need to bring in a "hired gun" to fill some knowledge gaps?

Pro Tip 17:

Don't let the pursuit of perfection become the nemesis of realizing excellence.[5]

Like everyone else, Enterprise Architects should always *strive* for perfection. However, at the risk of appearing trite, such an ideal remains tantalizingly unattainable.

Excellence, however, is not.

---

5 The original version of this quote which reads, "Don't let the perfect be the enemy of the good," is originally from *6 Habits That Hurt Your Career—and How to Overcome Them*, by Kerry Goyette.

EAs can't always build what they want—precisely. Unfortunately, they must address the practical realities of life: Schedules, budgets, capabilities, technological limitations, etc. Thus, EAs must remain pragmatic because every architecture will have its "seams," every design will have its "appendages," and every topology will have its "creases."

It's okay.

That said, however, never settle for anything less than *excellence*.

Pro Tip 18:

Take small bites of the apple.

There is no embarrassment in taking small steps when approaching a new challenge. Design in stages, build in stages, improve in stages.

As you proceed, you grow incrementally smarter, and refining prior work product is manageable. In the end, you'll be pleasantly surprised at the quality of the overall result.

The phrase, *stepwise refinement*, should become the mantra of every Enterprise Architect.

Pro Tip 19:

Stay current.

Can you imagine an Enterprise Architect who is not an ardent technologist?[6] Of course not. So, it wouldn't be surprising to discover that EAs spend a significant portion of their workweek evaluating and assessing technological trends. EAs love to do it, so it isn't a chore (for most, anyway).

But EAs should not limit their due diligence to the narrow vision of IT. Instead, they should expand their vistas and stay current with business developments (generally and specifically in the vertical markets they support), security issues (they affect everything), workforce trends (at heart, IT is still a people industry), etc.

Before being able to wield knowledge as power, one must acquire it.

---

6 Unfortunately, I've worked with a few.

Pro Tip 20:

> Support test teams.

Whether you agree with me or not, skilled[7] Test Engineers are the unsung heroes of most successful IT projects. They are the last line of protection, and their efforts can result in accolades—rather than embarrassment—when products deploy.

Make friends with them, take them to lunch, and defend them when other stakeholders berate them (when they deserve it).

Pro Tip 21:

> Always walk the cat backward.

Never gloss over defect mitigation. Band-Aids, gum, and paper clips will eventually lose their luster. Patches slip, hacks fail, and shortcuts always come back to haunt you (see Pro Tip 22).

Instead, always determine the root cause of *every* bug and fix *that*. Even if it means following the trail all the way back to its origin in a User Story. Otherwise, even the best designs will begin to bulge at the seams.

Pro Tip 22:

> You never have time for shortcuts.

I won't harp. Do it right the first time. You'll save time and money in the long run.

Pro Tip 23:

> If you don't know, say so.

Enterprise Architects should never guess.

---

7 Sadly, many Test Engineers are not that competent.

No one knows everything. When EAs act as if they do, they undermine their credibility and put projects at risk. Instead, when asked for any information of which they are ignorant or uncertain, EAs should respond by saying, "I don't know," and commit to researching the issue(s) and responding by a specific date. Then, obviously, the EA should follow through on every commitment (see Pro Tip 24).

Such integrity and commitment quickly develop credibility with stakeholders and team members.

Pro Tip 24:

Keep your word.

Think before you promise—then deliver. Every time. No excuses.

Pro Tip 25:

If you're an independent contractor, never say "no."

Saying "no" irks stakeholders and eventually opens the door to a potential replacement if uttered too frequently. It's far better to respond by saying, "Yes, but ..."

Pro Tip 26:

Stay calm.

To quote the famous actor Michael Caine, "Be a duck, remain calm on the surface, and paddle like hell underneath."[8]

Enterprise Architects should always project an air of conviction, confidence, and self-assurance—even when they suspect (or *know*) that their jobs/careers/reputations may hang in the balance. If they don't, EAs will surely lose the support of their colleagues and likely guarantee project and personal failure.

---

8 There are many versions of the maxim.

But it should go without saying that the EA in question better have what it takes to get the job done.

Pro Tip 27:

Don't be autocratic.

Given that there are often multiple approaches to addressing an issue, Enterprise Architects should solicit suggestions from all stakeholders. I believe that the more minds involved in solving a problem, the better the solution (committees aside).

When the time comes, the EA should present all options to the decision-makers. Indeed, EAs can—and should—suggest a preferred option. But always leave the door open to discussion.

SUMMARY

I hope this chapter highlighted the fact that those who serve as Enterprise Architects must view it as a starring role, not a cameo appearance. It requires a diverse set of skills—acting chief among them—and many virtues like dedication, patience, and persistence.

If, after reading this chapter, you conclude that the EA limelight is too hot, there is no need to worry. Although every role must have a player, not every performer is suitable for every part. It might take some time, but you'll find a stage upon which your star can shine.

However, if this profession does appeal to you, I urge you to pursue a career as an EA. Talented, dedicated Enterprise Architects are a valuable and scarce commodity.

8

What Causes Projects to Fail?

Programming is about managing complexity: the complexity of the problem laid upon the complexity of the machine. Because of this complexity, most of our programming projects fail.

—Bruce Eckel

The best way to get a project done faster is to start sooner.

—Jim Highsmith

INTRODUCTION

In this chapter, we will address the question: Why do IT projects fail?

As we will see, the reasons software development efforts fall short of expectations are numerous. Many of which are beyond the Enterprise Architect's control.

For example, I've served as the EA on projects canceled for the following reasons:

- A buyout or a merger (in-flight projects often get shelved to prevent duplication after the companies consolidate systems)
- Unforeseen budget cuts because of unexpected economic changes or substantial revenue shortfalls (companies must stop the financial bleeding to survive)
- A new regime takes control of the organization (as the saying goes, new brooms sweep clean)

DOI: 10.1201/9781003414285-8

Because these events are effectively *Deus ex machina*, Enterprise Architects can do little to create a "soft landing" for such ill-fated projects.

But that brings us to the main thrust of this chapter.

There are many reasons why projects fail that are *directly* related to the activities and responsibilities of EAs and other stakeholders. In the following sections, we will examine some of the most prevalent. Please note that I've culled all the examples discussed below from personal experience.

To simplify the presentation, I've grouped the issues under some general headings. That said, many of these topics could appear in multiple sections. In such cases, I chose the one I thought best categorized the problem.

Also, note that failed projects often suffer from more than one of the many issues described below. Sadly, there's no way to limit the scope of mismanagement.

However, before we dive too deeply into the underlying causes, we should take a moment to define what constitutes project failure.

WHAT DEFINES PROJECT FAILURE?

Henry Ford famously stated, "Failure is simply the opportunity to begin again, this time more intelligently."

The sentiment Mr. Ford expressed is true in the large, and we should all take it to heart personally. Nonetheless, it's of little consolation if, after working on a failed project, you find yourself unemployed and spending scads of time uploading your resume on numerous job-posting sites. Furthermore, it's usually challenging to convince a would-be future client/ employer that "I've failed at this task/position so many times before that I'm positive I'll get it right the next time working for you."

Interviewers would undoubtedly look askance when listening to such reasoning. Thus, at the risk of stating the obvious, when assuming responsibility for a project, most folks want it to succeed—for any number of reasons.

Nonetheless, about 65% of software projects fail.[1] Unfortunately, unless you're a professional baseball player, that's an appalling batting average.[2]

---

1 2020—The Standish Group International, Inc.
2 Baseball players who hit .350 are rare indeed.

But what constitutes failure? Most organizations use the following categories.

The project:

- Fell short of stakeholder objectives and expectations
- Failed to meet all its specified user requirements
- Required an excessive amount of time to complete (as compared to its projected schedule)
- Demanded resources far in excess of its proposed budget

Yes, some of these criteria are subjective (e.g., falling short of stakeholder expectations). Moreover, based on these vague metrics, many systems that ultimately "work" in Production might still constitute a failure. Nonetheless, the industry uses these metrics to set the bar.

In the following sections, we'll examine some underlying causes for this excessively high failure rate.

POOR PLANNING

When it comes to project planning, there are several quotes cited so often that they've become clichés.[3]

To wit:

Proper preparation prevents poor performance.

—Charlie Batch

—and—

He who fails to plan plans to fail.

—Emily Giffin

However, I believe the following quote by former US Secretary of Defense Robert McNamara more accurately expresses the idea.

---

3 This comment is not meant to demean them in any way. On the contrary, to its credit, an expression becomes clichéd because it precisely captures the essence of an idea.

Poor planning or poor execution of plans is simply to let some force other than reason shape reality.

With this in mind, let's explore how poor planning manifests itself in the SDLC.

Quixotic Scoping

Confession 1:

Many projects are poorly scoped.

Most often, the genesis of organizational initiatives results from one stakeholder's spark of genius: "Wouldn't it be great if we could—" This is the flash of entrepreneurial brilliance that fuels the engines of enterprise.

In most other disciplines—after experiencing the eureka moment—the next step is to analyze the problem/suggestion, determine its viability, establish its scope, and then develop an implementation plan. But unfortunately, stakeholders seem to discard such prudence when the idea involves software development. Indeed, in some cases, project patrons progress from conception to coding with little more than a sketch drawn on a cocktail napkin.

After all, it's just programming. So how hard could it possibly be?

For most large-scale development projects, planning requires significantly more time and effort than most stakeholders realize. Some of the more critical tasks include:

- Designing data models (in the form of enterprise schemas)
- Sketching UI designs (as a sequence of wireframes)
- Crafting requirements (often written as user stories)
- Establishing success criteria (as a series of measurable metrics)
- Defining test cases (specified as a set of preconditions, procedures, and postconditions)
- Engineering test data (to support both open-box and closed-box testing)

Unfortunately, none of the above tasks come from a squeeze bottle or a shrink-wrapped package. Nor can you order them as "development kits" from Amazon, downloaded "templates" from Wikipedia, or "acquire" them from previously completed projects.[4] Instead, architects, designers, and software engineers must craft them specifically for the task at hand, thus requiring effort, diligence, and creativity in their own right.

Regardless of the development methodology employed, eliminating any of the above steps (and some others not explicitly mentioned) undermines the definition and understanding of a project's scope and is, quite frankly, a recipe for disaster.

In other words: If you haven't specified your destination, how will you know when you've arrived?

Yes, during a project's pendency, its scope may change. (As I write this paragraph, I can't remember ever working on one that didn't.) But decision-makers should always fully understand the impact of any potential modification before consenting to it. However, the only way to assess its effect is to evaluate the benefits of a proposed alteration—and its accompanying costs and schedule impacts—against the original expectations.

Deficient Design

Confession 2:

Many projects are poorly designed.

Every human endeavor is a balancing act: How much investment (i.e., some combination of time, money, and resources) am I willing to invest to achieve a particular goal? For example, would it be appropriate to hire a modern-day Frank Lloyd Wright to construct a treehouse for your children? Alternatively, would it be prudent to assign a newly graduated software developer to design your organization's next-generation architecture?

Unfortunately, many organizations implicitly assume a variation of the latter approach when adopting the Agile methodology. Specifically, if they opt to forgo an initial design phase, they are, in effect, delegating that task to (potentially junior) programmers by allowing them to "work out the details." Moreover, many stakeholders believe it's best to get started quickly and then fix/adjust/tweak "on the fly."

---

4 Although you *can* leverage key learnings and acquired knowledge.

As highlighted earlier in the text, I describe this mindset as follows:

Project Goal	Travel to the moon.
First Step	Climb a tree because it gets us closer, then we'll figure out what to do next.

Adopting Agile—or any other rapid development methodology—is not an excuse to avoid or defer thinking. Indeed, as the above silly example demonstrates, without some initial thought—dare I say planning?—you might find yourself "out on a limb."

Despite protestations to the contrary and countless articles found in the literature, the fact remains that as they mature, poorly architected projects become:

- Difficult to maintain
- Challenging to scale
- Costly to extend

Once underway, few business stakeholders will sacrifice precious sprint resources "fixing" poor designs when they have "important" business features that "can't wait."

Pro Tip 1:

Take time to *think*.

As an Enterprise Architect, you will likely get only one opportunity to do your job correctly. Thus, if you expect a system to remain viable for an extended period, I strongly urge you to take the time to develop a professional-caliber architecture. I assure you that the ROI is more than worth it.

Romantic Deadlines

Most people—including myself—share the following attributes:

- They are always eager to start something new
- They often allow their initial enthusiasm to cloud their judgment

So, how do these characteristics affect IT projects?

Confession 3:

For many projects, deadlines are artificial.

Many stakeholders are overly optimistic during the preliminary stages of project planning (often called project scoping). As a result, it becomes tantalizingly easy to sit in front of a whiteboard and opine as follows:

We can complete Project 1 by this date, then follow on with Project 2 six months later, and …

The danger is that once the planning team establishes a completion date—even during a preliminary scoping phase—any modification to that timeframe becomes a "schedule slip." As a result, through no fault of the development team, the project will likely find itself on the failure side of the ledger if/when it completes.

What stakeholders often fail to consider when developing their initial "handwave" estimates are issues such as:

- Order-of-magnitude (i.e., WAGs[5]) estimates are usually wrong by as much as 50% (or more)
- Architects and software engineers rarely participate in scoping estimates
- The bottlenecks caused by competing resources, such as data center assets, operational staff shortages, purchase order cycles, logistical delays, and so on

Moreover, many stakeholders suffer from:

- A quaint belief that software is easy to create
- A whimsical conviction that all subcontractors and third-party providers always deliver on time
- A playful assumption that everyone loves change and will do nothing to thwart its progress

---

5 A WAG is a wild-ass-guess.

- A fanciful notion that new technology is easy to understand and simple to integrate into existing environments

What's particularly frustrating to developers—who rarely get to work a "normal" day under the best of circumstances—are project managers who think nothing of altering requirements in response to changing business needs but only grudgingly consider altering delivery dates. In my experience, it's never the project managers who have to work 18-hour days to prevent a schedule slip.

Pro Tip 2:

Include the technology team during the project formulation stage.

Including "techies" during the project scoping phase will produce more reasonable—if less palatable—schedules and estimates.

Machiavellian Politics

As a project expands in scope (from local to enterprise), its difficulties grow proportionally. Moreover, as the number of groups involved with or affected by a project increases, the political implications increase exponentially.

Confession 4:

Politics is not the sole province of government or C-level executives.

Every organization of any appreciable size develops factions, and their leaders feel compelled to grow their fiefdoms—it's just human nature. And unfortunately, part of that process is wielding influence which, in turn, causes organizational conflict.

I know, you're shocked.

Consequently, that means Enterprise Architects might experience any or all of the following on any given project:

- Leader A does not like—or could feel threatened by—Leader B and thus might actively obstruct any projects that are the brainchild of—or will benefit—Leader B
- A group might believe their livelihood is in jeopardy if a given project succeeds and will thus thwart its progress at every turn
- Leader A is a megalomaniac and will fight for control of every high-visibility project
- Projects that span multiple groups will likely have stakeholders that offer conflicting, sometimes sincere, opinions about what's best for the organization

Resolving such internal conflicts is wearisome, drains resources, and affects project expectations. Sadly, I've worked at some companies—not for very long, mind you—whose organizational in-fighting was so vicious and so destructive that very few projects saw the light of day.

Pro Tip 3:

Enterprise Architects should avoid politics to the extent possible. But when forced to engage, they should do so impartially, espousing what's best for the organization in the large, not an individual fiefdom.

Haphazard Triage

Given infinite time and unlimited resources, Enterprise Architects could design and build the most astounding systems.

Alas, I don't know anyone fortunate enough to have been part of such a project.

Confession 5:

As the old saying goes, if everything is a priority, then nothing is a priority.

Unfortunately, finances, time, and patience are finite and limited resources on this planet. Thus, every project team will eventually confront the following question:

We have ten pounds of "stuff" and only a five-pound bag. What should we do?

In a perfect world, Project Managers would have addressed and resolved such issues long before arriving at such a crossroads. Alas, if only that were true because disagreements on development priorities can cause raging disputes regarding what items to include "in the bag."

Unfortunately, for some stakeholders, if the feature decisions are not to their liking, they will become disgruntled and disappointed, labeling the project a failure. Indeed, some may actively thwart its success. But, of course, they will do this only after stomping their feet, pounding their desks, and holding their breath until turning blue in the face.

Pro Tip 4:

Include the technical team when performing feature triage because they can often group requirements in ways that allow the best bang for the limited development dollar.

User Indifference

In my experience, the following two confessions seem to occur as a pair.

Confession 6:

In many project teams, the user is the last consideration.

Confession 7:

Many stakeholders don't realize there are many classes of users.

In his 1922 book, *My Life and Work*, Henry Ford may have epitomized customer indifference when he wrote:

> Therefore in 1909, I announced one morning, without any previous warning, that in the future, we were going to build only one model, that the model was going to be "Model T," and that the chassis would be exactly the same for all cars, and I remarked: "Any customer can have a car painted any colour [sic] that he wants so long as it is black."

Though not as extreme, this attitude toward addressing users' needs is still prevalent today, especially during a schedule crunch.

Please consider the following examples I've culled from personal experience:

- A system that is so ineffective that users effectively replace it with a spreadsheet they share privately via email
- An application so poorly designed that it requires manual processing to bridge feature gaps
- A UI that doesn't anticipate the user's next processing step

Unfortunately, many project teams forget that users are their *raison d'etre*. Indeed, I can't tell you how often I've heard hard-working programmers complain about the pedestrian and mindless code they must develop, forgetting that they'd be out-of-work programmers if it weren't for that pedestrian and mindless code.

Another glaring misstep is that system designers often forget that there are many classes of users. For example, they often overlook the needs of managers, operation staff, and even future maintenance programmers.

As a result, they neglect to include actionable alerts, useful diagnostic and log messages, intelligible status displays, and adequate documentation—all of which are foundational elements of a professional-caliber system.

Pro Tip 5:

Validate every decision based on how it affects every class of user.

Unfortunately, not all programming can be the slick, flashy, state-of-the-art coding that challenges, energizes, and motivates developers. Nonetheless, it must always remain laser-focused on addressing the needs of the user communities.

Confession 8:

> User indifference engenders lackluster applications that create more problems than they solve.

Enigmatic Objectives

It might seem counterintuitive, but not all institutional knowledge should remain proprietary. Indeed, contrary to tradition and expectation, C-level executives are not the only stakeholders who need information to function effectively.

Confession 9:

> Withholding knowledge is the *sine qua non* for most organizations.

Playing "close to the vest" works very well for poker players, but it's not the best approach when dealing with the individuals responsible for shaping an organization's future. In addition to direction, they need information. The more, the better.

Surprisingly, one of the most significant handicaps to project success isn't overcoming technical hurdles or disambiguating confusing requirements. Instead, it's widespread ignorance of organizational objectives on behalf of project teams, which leads to poor business decisions.

Confession 10:

> Many organizations treat development staff like mushrooms: They're kept in the dark, covered in manure.

Many folks don't consider this, but every choice a developer makes constitutes a business decision, not a technical one.

Why?

Every decision a software engineer makes has immediate repercussions on budgets and schedules, not to mention the long-term impacts on future system maintenance and extensibility. Given that every coding choice has broad implications, it would greatly benefit projects if every programmer shared the same decision-making framework. Unfortunately, when kept ignorant of organizational objectives, developers—like most human beings—will often "take the easy way out," which frequently leads to less-than-optimal solutions.

Confession 11:

Many organizations are unaware of the benefits of developing a Business Architecture.

One way to establish organizational direction and disseminate it to the appropriate staff is by developing and maintaining a Business Architecture. This process not only firmly plants a stake in the ground, but like a lighthouse, it serves as a directional beacon for every decision—large and small.

Pro Tip 6:

Develop a formal Business Architecture and disseminate it to all project team members.

Siloed Environments

Most organizations subdivide themselves into sectors, variously called divisions, business units, departments, regions, etc. And, as noted above, because information is power, they refuse to share it with others and play nicely in the sandbox.

Confession 12:

Most organizational subdivisions suffer from the NIH[6] Syndrome: They firmly believe that if they didn't build it, it isn't any good, and they shouldn't use it.

A siloed mentality is in direct conflict with enterprise-wide solutions and thwarts the ability to achieve critical organizational goals successfully.

How is this an example of poor planning?

When individual siloes are left to their own devices, solutions become:

- Duplicated
- Narrowly focused
- Costly to build (i.e., no economies of scale)
- Misaligned with enterprise directives
- Technology-laden (i.e., duplicate/overlapping products and components)
- Prone to data hoarding
- Challenging to integrate
- Confusing to the user community
- Difficult to operate and maintain

Comprehensive planning at the enterprise level can render most of these issues moot.

Errors of Omission vs. Errors of Commission

All of us are subject to missteps, gaffs, and outright blunders. That goes without saying. Broadly speaking, there are two major classes of mistakes: Errors of *commission* and errors of *omission*.

Errors of *commission* are the type of mistakes most associated with the human condition. For example, we misread an instruction, execute the wrong command, or misunderstand a directive. We've all been there, and despite our best efforts, we'll be there again.

Errors of *omission* are entirely another matter, however. These gaffs occur when project team members knowingly and deliberately avoid or

---

6 Not Invented Here.

sidestep tasks usually associated with professional competency. In other words, indolence overcomes diligence.

Confession 13:

> Errors of omission are far more prevalent and pernicious than most senior executives would imagine.

How does such indolence manifest? Some examples follow.

- When stakeholders don't thoroughly vet new technologies during the planning phase, project-impacting issues might result so late in the schedule that it severely limits mitigation strategies.
- Results can radically diverge from expectations when requirements don't undergo rigorous review.
- When project managers deliberately forgo unit testing (as a way to manage schedules), system quality suffers dramatically.

As this is an innately human condition, there is no cure, only a treatment. Thus, for the Enterprise Architect, I'd like to reprise a Pro Tip that will help address this issue.

Pro Tip 7:

> Trust, but verify.

INADEQUATE REQUIREMENTS

Please recall this quote from a previous chapter.

Walking on water and developing software from a specification are both easy if both are frozen.—Edward V. Bernard

One of the most common causes of project failure is inadequate requirements. Indeed, specifications establish a formal agreement about expectations: Project designers codify their vision; programmers realize the dream.

As the above quote so eloquently suggests, a project's success directly correlates to the clarity and solidity of its requirements.

The following sections will explore how shortchanging the requirements effort can affect project success.

Vague User Stories

One benchmark of a well-designed software algorithm is the predictability and repeatability of its results. Similarly, this metric should also serve as a touchstone for evaluating the quality of user stories. Specifically, if a user story is subject to multiple—and potentially—conflicting interpretations, I would argue that stakeholders should not consider development staff responsible for the inevitable pushback from users during acceptance testing.

Confession 14:

Vague requirements are shockingly the norm and are a significant cause of project failure.

Would you ever expect to see a blueprint for a house containing a specification that reads, "We'll position a window somewhere along the back wall?" Most of us would expect the construction team to balk at such a vague directive.

Yet, in IT projects, it's not uncommon for stakeholders—including the development team—to allow such ambiguous requirements. They frequently perform a handwave and say something like, "We'll work out the details later."

They rarely do.

Pro Tip 8:

Review requirements and system specifications carefully.

As noted above, a well-written user story should yield one, and only one, interpretation.

Scope Creep

Scope creep is another significant contributor to project failure. To get us started, let's begin with a definition.

Definition 1:

> Scope creep—also called requirements creep—occurs when a project undergoes unrestrained expansion or modification of its specifications.

The causes of scope creep are numerous, some of which are actually valid.

Increased Knowledge	Individuals and project teams grow more knowledgeable with time. And because ingenuity doesn't occur on a schedule, we can only incorporate ideas when they come to light.
Environmental Changes	Because they are beyond their control, organizations must react to changes in the business environment as they occur.
Fear of Saying "No"	Sometimes, the most appropriate response to a change request is "no." Justifications for rejecting a requirement modification include the following:

- It's too costly
- It's too time-consuming
- It would undermine the architecture
- The "ripple effects" are too extensive

Political Issues	Organizational politics are real and unavoidable. Sadly, sometimes folks force changes simply to establish "who's boss."

When scope changes are unavoidable, stakeholders should undertake the following safeguards.

Adherence to Objectives	Many late-breaking requirements don't align with a project's original objectives. Therefore, stakeholders should conduct formal reviews of all proposed modifications to ensure they support, and are in furtherance of, the project's goals.
Good Communication	Change can't happen in a vacuum. All stakeholders need to be made aware of all specification changes.
Change Management	Stakeholders should track all requirements changes and record their implications and impacts.

Confession 15:

Because it typically originates with checkbook-wielding stakeholders, scope creep often goes unchallenged.

To fully appreciate its implications, we need to understand the full scope of scope creep.

Specifically, it's one thing to change an icon's image, the position of a screen control, or the constraints on a business rule. However, even most Agile-based organizations can't readily react and recalibrate when requirement changes affect application architecture, database schemas, or infrastructure topology.

Some of the consequences of unfettered scope creep include the following:

- Increased technical debt
- Schedule slips
- Budget impacts
- Original feature reduction
- Backlog expansion

Pro Tip 9:

> To restrain scope creep, develop strong technical and financial arguments that clearly articulate their impact.

Do your best to prevent the changes. Then, after you lose the argument, do your best to implement them.

Conflicting Priorities

Project teams function best when they understand organizational priorities. For example, developers can determine the best sequence for implementing low-level functions, Database Administrators (DBAs) can anticipate schema extensions, and operations staff can decide the most appropriate hardware delivery and installation schedules.

Confession 16:

> Many project planners prioritize features "on the fly."

When planners don't prioritize features, the efforts of the project's various designers and implementers may not align. The resulting confusion leads to chaos, conflicting priorities, and project failure.

Pro Tip 10:

> Planners should plan.

Forgetting the User

Whether constructing a custom, in-house system or developing a third-party retail application, the user community should remain front and center. But unfortunately, this is not always the case within some organizations.

Confession 17:

In many IT shops, the "user" is only a vague concept.

Like the child's game "telephone," requirements morph as they move farther away from users. Thus, development shops often build less-than-optimal solutions for the problems they are addressing. However, it's not always the development team's fault, especially in organizations that isolate them. (Please see the section below entitled The Business Analyst.)

Pro Tip 11:

Enterprise Architects should ensure every technical and project decision has the user in mind.

INADEQUATE ARCHITECTURE

If you think good architecture is expensive, try bad architecture.

—Brian Foote

As I've mentioned throughout this book and again underscored in Confession 17, many stakeholders—including IT professionals—discount the value and benefit of enterprise architecture. Indeed, these very individuals—many of whom wouldn't even consider grilling a chicken wing without a comprehensive recipe—wouldn't think twice about forgoing a project's planning stage so they can "get coding."

Confession 18:

There is never enough time for shortcuts.

Enterprise Architecture—whether planned or *ad hoc*—can persist for *generations*. So, whether it's allocated as a specific line item in a project's budget or its costs span scores of sprints, every development shop must fund system design efforts.

Ultimately, you have a choice: You can either pay upfront or as you go—but you will pay. And as we will see in subsequent sections, it usually costs far more when you defer payment.

Haphazard Design

Many seasoned developers will appreciate this story. A client hired me to replace a project's senior architect. (The reasons are irrelevant.) After getting my bearings (e.g., reading design documents, reviewing requirements, and assessing code), I triaged the technical debt and allocated assignments to individual developers.

I considered one problem a "slam dunk" to solve, so I delegated it to a junior programmer. To my great dismay, a week passed, and the task was still "open." When I asked the programmer for an update, he responded by recounting the litany of code changes he had already completed and those he still had to finish to close out the ticket. So, of course, my initial reaction was, "This guy is too 'green' and is solving nonexistent problems."[7]

But sadly, I was wrong.

As it turned out, the system and data architectures were so convoluted that this simple change required modifying at least ten modules and multiple database tables.[8] It took that developer almost another week to close the ticket—through no fault of his.

Confession 19:

> Many organizations hide the impact of poor system design during project maintenance cycles.

There are many ways that poor design can "come back to haunt you." Four of the most significant appear below.

---

7 As an aside, this programmer turned out to be one of the best developers I ever had the privilege of working with.
8 This is an example of "paying later."

Cascading Changes	As the anecdote I shared at the beginning of this section highlighted, poor design can require modifications that span many modules and multiple system components. Such convoluted changes are challenging to complete in and of themselves. However, they also increase testing costs (e.g., unit, system, integration, performance, and acceptance), documentation revision, and updates to design specifications.
Lack of Reuse	The more convoluted the design, the less likely programmers will reuse existing code, modules, components, and services. Consequently, systems will invariably develop duplicate code, thus increasing future maintenance costs even more.
Break on Fix	Break on fix is far more prevalent in poorly designed systems. This problem is another example of a "soft cost" that can remain hidden from even the most vigilant senior executives who are not "tech savvy."
Design Appendages	One crucial measure of any architecture is its ability to support even extensive changes in ways that maintain the existing design. In other words, a well-designed system accommodates change from within, not as a series of external appendages.

Maybe I'm off base, but I believe deliberately hiding such soft costs from senior management is tantamount to malpractice.

Missing Roadmap

When traveling without a pre-planned route, how do you know whether the information you receive from real-time traffic reports will eventually affect your arrival time? The obvious answer is that you don't. Such information becomes "white noise" that ultimately annoys more than it helps.

So how does this little anecdote relate to inadequate architecture?

Sometimes, due to forces beyond their control, project teams must change gears, modify routes, and contend with detours. But without a preexisting baseline, how do stakeholders understand how unexpected events affect a project's costs and schedules?

Confession 20:

Many organizations don't appreciate that, absent a formal enterprise architecture to cushion them from changes in the wind, even a gentle breeze will alter their route.

Systems developed without the benefit of an Enterprise Architecture are subject to any/all of the following:

- Replicated code/services
- Integration difficulties
- Data anomalies
- Costly maintenance/extension
- User rejection/pushback
- Poor performance/reliability

If you don't believe me, you might consider the warning put forward by Winston Churchill, who said, "He <sic> who fails to plan is planning to fail."

Misaligned Enterprise Architecture

Would you expect similar designs for houses built in the tropics and Antarctica?

Of course, not.

On the contrary, you'd assume the blueprints for each structure reflect the demands of the intended environment.

So, why do Enterprise Architects ignore environmental factors when designing systems?

Confession 21:

> Many Enterprise Architects fail to incorporate their organization's goals into their designs.

Enterprise Architects must tailor designs to the business sector, locality, and objectives of the organization for whom they ply their trade. Thus, by definition, enterprise architecture is *bespoke*, not "off the shelf."

I've seen many cases where EAs have mechanically applied solution "patterns" rather than designing custom solutions *based* on patterns.

In my opinion, this is also tantamount to malpractice.

Failing to Reassess

Unlike building designs that may remain unchanged for scores—if not hundreds—of years, Enterprise Architectures are always subject to modification and extension. Shifts in technology, business projections, organizational goals, marketplace considerations, etc., all drive change. Thus, in response, Enterprise Architects should periodically revise, revamp, or extend their designs as appropriate.

Confession 22:

> Many Enterprise Architects adhere to the "fire and forget" rule.

To be clear, I'm not suggesting that EAs modify their architectures in response to every article appearing in technical journals. Nor am I proposing that organizations redesign systems in response to the revenues posted in their most recent quarterly report.

Instead, I recommend that EAs regularly (e.g., every two to three years) formally reassess the viability of their designs based on environmental shifts and adjustments to organizational goals. Small periodic tweaks applied meticulously will go a long way to ensuring an excellent ROI for all the expense and effort expended on architectural design and infrastructure buildout.

Shortchanging the "Ilities"

As you may recall from Chapter 6, I use the term "ilities" to refer to design attributes such as availability, reliability, and testability. They are all critical design elements that Enterprise Architects cannot ignore.

Confession 23:

> Many Enterprise Architects defer consideration of the "ilities" until it's too late in the project lifecycle to mitigate any resulting issues.

I've seen many projects that have uncovered alarming security, performance, and availability shortcomings during the integration test phase. Consequently, as you might imagine, the mitigation techniques employed at this stage often rely on mallets and axes rather than tacking hammers and scalpels.

Confession 24:

> Some Enterprise Architects don't know how to integrate the "ilities" into their designs. Thus, they can't possibly demonstrate how their approach meets or exceeds the system's non-functional requirements.

What's worse than the lack of professionalism reflected in Confession 24, I've worked with not one but two Enterprise Architects who avoided including some "ilities" because they affected the *aesthetic quality* of their designs. That is, they eliminated some of the "ilities" because it made their drawings look "messy."

Yikes!

Professional EAs should address and incorporate these attributes into their designs from the outset. Moreover, EAs must demonstrate that their architectures will meet the Service Level Agreement (SLA) specified in the non-functional requirements *before* developers write their first lines of code.

DISMAL TEAM COMPOSITION

Get the right people. Then no matter what all else you might do wrong after that, the people will save you. That's what management is all about.

—**Tom DeMarco**

To say my fate is not tied to your fate is like saying, "Your end of the boat is sinking."

—**Hugh Downs**

In real estate, the oft-repeated mantra is *location, location, location*. However, in IT—and most other human endeavors, for that matter—the chant one should employ is *people, people, people*.

When discussing a software project's likelihood of success, you can dismiss the impacts of technology, requirements, methodologies, and the like. Because, in the end, it boils down to people: Talented teams succeed; incompetent groups fail.

Yes, tools do help. However, even using primitive implements, *professionals* will always produce exceptional results. If you doubt my position, I suggest you visit any museum and behold the staggering array of historical artwork created using tools that today's artists might consider primitive. Yet, most would take your breath away.

In the following sections, we will discuss some issues regarding team composition.

Too Little Staff

You can't put ten pounds of flour into a five-pound sack. (Earlier in the text, I expressed this caveat another way.) This admonition applies to teams: You can't expect a five-person team to produce as much work product as a ten-person team.

I'm sorry, but like sacks and flour, the math doesn't work.

Confession 25:

> Most stakeholders expect development staff to overcome every unexpected event and all planning, estimating, and technological deficiencies.

Despite everything you may have heard, developers are not seraphic beings, high-tech superheroes, or members of the *cognoscenti*. Instead, they are mere mortals. As such, they are subject to all the flaws, faults, and foibles associated with the human condition.

This includes burnout.

Developers understand crunch time; it's part of the job. Indeed, most are willing to go the extra mile with little more than a tankful of caffeine and the occasional late-night rest-stop pizza. However, asking too few programmers to do too much work in too little time is as unfair as it is unrealistic.

Team-building moments and feigned *esprit de corps* only go so far. I've rarely seen projects operating under such working conditions succeed. On the contrary, they are usually late and bug-ridden.

So, what works?

Project Managers who manage stakeholder expectations, place realistic demands on development teams, and propose reasonable schedules that include some "wiggle room" should the "flour" ever hit the fan.

That's what works.

Increasing Staff Size

In his 1975 book, *The Mythical Man-Month*, Fred Brooks famously noted, "adding manpower [sic] to a late software project makes it later."

Confession 26:

> The only thing you achieve when you add staff to floundering projects is to place additional demands on the existing team members.

Like many of life's observations, Mr. Brook's assertion seems counterintuitive. Nonetheless, it's true.

Newcomers need guidance. That guidance does not float in the ether—it must come from someone. Thus, in the short run, the existing staff becomes *less* productive because they must cater to the needs of the newbies.

Pro Tip 12:

Resist the urge to increase team size when mitigating schedule delays.

Before adding new members to your team, make sure you have enough runway available to regain any lost momentum so that the increased drag caused by the added staff won't prevent your project from taking off.

Otherwise, make do with what you have and adjust schedules accordingly.

Too Much Staff

Okay, you're smart and strive never to make the same mistake twice. Thus, once burned by the perils caused by an understaffed project team, you're twice shy and therefore decide to overcompensate by demanding a plethora of programmers (as well as testers, network engineers, DBAs, etc.).

Good move?

Not as good as you might think. Unfortunately, more is not always merrier.

Confession 27:

Project managers who hoard development resources usually find that their projects collapse under their own weight.

Again, although it seems counterintuitive, it's nonetheless true. So, to make my point, I'd like to begin by defining an economics theory called the Network Effect.

Definition 2:

The Network Effect describes a situation wherein current group members gain incremental benefits when new users join.

A perfect example of this phenomenon occurred during the salad days of the then-burgeoning telephone network. As more consumers acquired telephones, existing users could "reach out and touch"[9] more and more individuals.

As highlighted by the above example, in the business world, the impacts of the Network Effect are usually positive. However, this does not always hold in the realm of IT system development.

Consider that as you add individuals to a team, the number of potential interactions increases dramatically. Moreover, as the development staff grows, so do the coordination, management, and oversight issues. This, in turn, demands more meetings, increased supervision, and further planning, thus reducing individual productivity.

As we all learned long ago, a complimentary lunch is never free. In this case, the increased management overhead burdens projects and affects their success.

Pro Tip 13:

Try to right-size your projects.

Too Much Collaboration

Well-designed software is modular with well-defined interfaces. This design approach limits component interaction to a specific set of (hopefully) well-designed touch points.

Project managers should adopt and apply this technique to project management.

Confession 28:

Most projects convene too many meetings with too many attendees addressing too many topics resulting in too little progress.

---

9 In the 1970s, the Bell System (one of the major telephone service providers at the time) used this phrase as part of an advertising campaign.

Writing software is a heads-down undertaking requiring significant concentration for extended periods. Indeed, programmers must often "juggle" large quantities of information when coding. As a result, developers refer to interruptions as "popping the stack."[10] (If you've coded, no explanation for this reference is necessary. If you haven't, no description will be adequate.)

Suffice it to say that unnecessary meetings—or required attendance in unproductive, unfocused, unwarranted "gatherings"—affect developer productivity.

Period. Full stop.

I don't just mean the time wasted sitting in an airless conference room listening to Business Analysts droning on about the relative benefits of some proposed UI modification when one of them could have simply *asked* the users and then shared their observations with the development team in a brief, concise email.

No, this isn't bad enough.

I'm also referring to the time programmers require to "repopulate their mental stacks" when they finally get to return to their desks and resume working. This scenario is yet another example of a soft cost that, in most cases, developers must "absorb" if they are to honor their schedule commitments.

Pro Tip 14:

Don't waste developer time.

Too Little Collaboration

We've all witnessed it from the safety of our project's hunting blinds: Rogue developers sneaking off to stalk their own objectives regardless of the intentions of the pack leaders. Moreover, these lone predators seem to "know better" than all other team members and therefore feel justified in ignoring any groupthink findings.

---

10 A "stack" is a data structure developers use to maintain application state. When you "pop" the stack, you lose that state data.

Confession 29:

Every project seems to have at least one rogue developer.

As mentioned in the prior section, software development is a solitary discipline. But wait, so is sculling. Yet, if all the oars-persons don't row in a coordinated manner, their boat will likely move in circles—if at all.

The same holds with IT projects. Even if the heading is less than optimal, projects can only progress apace when every team member paddles in the same direction.

For example, I'd like to have a dollar for every time a developer insisted they had discovered a better component/tool/library/database/language/ API than the one selected for some aspect of the project. But unfortunately, they fail to realize (or, in my opinion, choose to ignore) that adopting the suggested utility might not be viable even if their technical assessment is accurate because of integration difficulties, licensing considerations, support concerns, performance issues, etc. What's worse, in many cases, these rogue developers often incorporate their tool *du jour* without the knowledge or consent of the team's technical leadership.

Please don't get the wrong idea. I'm not suggesting that project managers and technical leads inhibit ingenuity or curb creativity. On the contrary, they should welcome and encourage contributions from every team member.

But I am suggesting that such decisions can't occur in a vacuum.

As I mentioned earlier in this text, *all* decisions are business decisions. Thus, by definition, technical options—such as tool adoption—must be made in context and align with the organization's goals and objectives.

Missing Interpersonal Skills

Because software programming is a solitary endeavor, it attracts solitary individuals who often prefer to pursue solitary endeavors. At first blush, this seems like the perfect match.

But system development is a team effort requiring human interaction, personnel management, and project leadership.

Confession 30:

> In IT, many project managers and technical leads lack interpersonal skills.

Although I think many stakeholders (managers and developers alike) would prefer it, you can't toss a set of use cases "over the transom" and expect developers to deliver you a perfect system. Unfortunately, it doesn't work that way. Indeed, there's not enough fairy dust and wizard oil to produce such alchemy.

On the contrary, team members often need encouragement, coaching, understanding, disciplining, training, etc. Projects whose leaders lack the skills to recognize and address such issues are doomed to fail.

Deadwood

In every group endeavor, there are, by definition, some individuals whose talents don't shine as brightly as those of the team's stars. There's no need to carp or debate the point. For good or ill, that's how it is when dealing with human beings—not everyone excels at every task.

However, there is "not as productive," and there is "deadwood."

Confession 31:

> In most large-scale development projects, the stellar performers often must compensate for the productivity eclipse caused by a few dark stars.

For me, the worst types of deadwood are individuals whose sole motivation is to demonstrate their intelligence rather than simply contributing ideas for the team's betterment.

Pro Tip 15:

> When identified, replace deadwood with mighty oaks or some sturdy saplings whenever possible.

Lack of Talent

I've saved the most crucial attribute—talent—for last.

Genius has its limitations; stupidity has none.

—Dr. Brooks F. Beebe

The trouble with programmers is that you can never tell what a programmer is doing until it's too late.

—Seymour Cray

I don't care how much you *try*. I don't care how much you *work*. I don't care how much you *care*. Because, in the end, only results matter. And the weight of success usually rests on the shoulders of talent.

Confession 32:

> The best methodologies, technologies, topologies, and any other related "ologies" you can imagine won't overcome a lack of ability.

Again, sorry, not sorry.

Small teams comprising talented, dedicated, and motivated individuals succeed far more often than their large ponderous uninspired counterparts.

The effects caused by a lack of talent are especially evident in system test shops because many project managers "hide" their poorest performers in them. To compound the problem, as alluded to above, these organizations may also lack the "soft skills," resources, and incentives required to manage and develop employees.

Consequently, individuals who find themselves "hidden away" eventually realize their predicament and lose the remaining remnants of their pride and motivation, resulting in a sad state of affairs for both the testers and their applications.

TECHNOLOGY SHORTCOMINGS

Never trust a computer you can't throw out a window.

—Steve Wozniak.

Technology is at once fast-moving, breathtaking, life-altering, lifesaving, challenging, frustrating, pricey, inexpensive, awe-inspiring, timesaving, entertaining … okay, I'll stop here.

But the one thing technology is not is perfect.

Many IT stakeholders—including architects, designers, and developers—believe that the newest and greatest innovations will cure all ills. I can sum up their approach as follows:

> Hey, all we have to do is incorporate the latest <insert the technological component of choice>, and we can move on to the next problem after lunch.

If only it were that easy.

It would be impossible for me to recall how many meetings I've attended during which one or more participants parroted a marketing blurb they read that very morning about some brand-spanking new product that would address our application's performance issues, cut operating costs by 50%, and cure world hunger.

I find such gratuitous suggestions infuriating for several reasons. First and foremost, they were calculated. That is, the talking heads offered them simply as a means to engage in self-aggrandization.[11] They have zero hands-on experience with the product and no way to determine from a glance at its advertising copy whether it would genuinely serve the organization's needs.

Second, because the talking heads often piqued the interest of technology-challenged project managers, I, or my team members, would have to conduct costly due diligence to counter the suggestion. It would be impossible for me to estimate how much money (number of participants * length of discussions/reviews * average hourly salary * overhead expenses, etc.) organizations waste chasing technological rainbows.

---

11 Please refer to the section entitled *Deadwood*, above.

Such "visionaries" fail to realize that new is not necessarily better. Indeed, like hammers, open MRI machines, and synthetic building materials, all forms of technology are tools and, as such, are subject to failures, shortcomings, and misuse. And unlike changing the batteries in a universal remote, integrating a new piece of technology into an existing system design usually requires far more effort than a hand wave: There are learning curves, testing costs, integration issues, etc.

In this section, we'll discuss how technology itself can affect project success.

Designing for Technology

Who doesn't like something new and shiny?

I know I do.

Moreover, who wouldn't want to add another notch under the "experience" heading on their resumes?

I know I would.

But as Enterprise Architects, we can't let the glint and sparkle of a newly forged tool distract us from what should remain our primary focus: The users. We have a professional and fiduciary responsibility to our clients and employers. We must serve the stakeholders, not the technology.

Confession 33:

Many Enterprise Architects focus on technology and fail to keep the user centered in their design crosshairs.

As soon as Enterprise Architects start designing for technology instead of addressing the end-users' needs, they jeopardize the project's success. Tools and technology are a means to an end. However, they are by no means an end unto themselves.

Flawed Technology Selection

In almost every technological category, there are multiple product offerings. Moreover, in addition to the products, the categories themselves are often fungible.

Confession 34:

Many organizations don't provide adequate resources for their design teams to conduct satisfactory product evaluations.

A classic example is Database Management Systems. Consider that there are many classes of DBMS: relational, hierarchical, NoSQL, object-oriented, network, etc. And within each of these categories, there are multiple product offerings.

As more and more executives are discovering, data are their organizations' crown jewels. Given its significance, one can't overemphasize the importance of selecting the best category/product to host and maintain such a valuable resource. So how can decision-makers determine which offerings will best serve their organization's needs now and in the future?

The difficulty of answering that question is directly proportional to its consequences. But let me assure you, you won't find the solution in any advertising copy.

This type of formal evaluation requires the following high-level tasks:

- Identifying Business Drivers—define the organization's goals
- Requirements Specification—both functional and non-functional
- Candidate Identification—initial choice of products to receive
- Preparation of Tests—develop tests and testing data
- Product Testing—conduct trials
- Results Analysis—chose the winner

Unfortunately, even this level of due diligence does not *guarantee* the long-term viability of the winner. In addition to the usual variables—changes in the market, competitive practices, user preferences, etc.—you might find that your product of choice will start to show its seams over time. But don't take it to heart because even the best Enterprise Architects can't predict the future.

What's worse, however, is that you may discover that none of the currently available products in some category meets all your needs. Consequently, you might thus find yourself standing at an unexpected and undesirable crossroads.

At that point, do you:

- Buy the "best option currently available" and use it as is, despite its shortcomings
- Buy the "best option currently available" and modify it (assuming the licensing permits it)
- Roll our own (possibly from scratch or leveraging an open-source solution as a baseline)

Nonetheless, despite the tough decision now confronting you, having undertaken the due diligence effort ensures that you will at least make an informed decision.

One final comment. I'm not suggesting that every technological choice requires the level of due diligence described above. After all, a DBMS is a centerpiece, and its selection requires a commensurate level of evaluation. However, I suggest that every choice undergo a review proportional to its significance to the project and the organization.

Not Ready for Primetime

Confession 35:

Many Enterprise Architects believe that *new* is new better.

New is great, but EAs should remain skeptical and evaluate innovative products with a jaundiced eye. You don't want to be the customer who's told, "Oh yeah, that's a known bug, but the fix won't be available until next year."

Pro Tip 16:

I recommend not using a new product or a new version of an existing product until it has sufficient flight time to ensure that it flies smoothly. Instead, let beta testers and early adopters serve as test pilots.

As alluded to in the prior section, not every newly released product, tool, or component is ready for primetime. That's because there's only so much testing even the most respected development shops can afford to conduct.

As a result, even the best software houses can't anticipate how their applications will perform in all target environments until early adopters begin using the product and providing feedback in the form of bug reports, support requests, and in the worst cases, license cancellations.

Betting on the Wrong Company

Startups are great: They have new ideas/products, need your business, are willing to "turn on a dime," and are eager to prioritize new feature development for early adopters.

But how long will they be around?

Confession 36:

Many organizations fail to employ adequate precautions when relying on startups.

Estimates vary, but 75%–90% of new startups fail. Consequently, regardless of the exact percentage, the team marketing your newfangled product will likely not be around that long.

So, who will provide support, training, and bug fixes when they're gone?

Pro Tip 17:

Never rely on products offered by startups unless the company is willing to place its source code in escrow and make it available to customers in the event of their demise.

When working with software components offered by startups, you must accept that, at some point, you might need to support the product in-house.

POOR PROJECT MANAGEMENT

Expect the best, plan for the worst, and prepare to be surprised.

—Denis Waitley

Project management is both a skill and an art. Project Managers (PMs)—I mean good PMs—possess the talent and ability to combine disparate pieces into a unified whole and deliver *solutions* to stakeholders.

When done well, talented, professional PMs make it look easy—like they're not even there. However, when done poorly, projects quickly devolve into chaos as independent factions and rogue developers destroy any chance of success from within.

Most of the time, project management is akin to herding cats.

Let's review some of the challenges.

Control Issues

Imagine while in the middle of a long drive, your car's navigation system continually recomputed the route you were following for no apparent reason. That would get pretty annoying, right?

Now consider a similar scenario occurring during IT projects. That is, what would be the effect on the development staff if Program Managers continually shift objectives and change course? Do you think the project teams might lose their focus and direction?

Confession 37:

Many Project Managers don't know how to say "no."

PMs who don't manage change allow change to manage their projects. And when change manages projects, projects fail.

Fuzzy Roles

You may have heard of the term Fuzzy Logic (FL). FL is a logical reasoning model developed to address vague or imprecise statements. In addition, FL closely aligns with the Theory of Fuzzy Sets (FS), which applies to groups of related objects that lack clearly defined boundaries.

FL and FS mimic how we, as humans, deal with imprecise statements and definitions. Thus, their "fuzziness" and "fluid boundaries" are advantages, not detriments. As a result, they create robust conceptual models with many applications, from developing new consumer products to implementing Decision Support Systems (DSS).

However, such fuzziness should never be the case with IT projects.

Confession 38:

> Many Program Managers allow too much role overlap in their project teams.

When role definitions are "fuzzy," so are the resulting decisions. When decisions are confusing, conflicting, or contradictory, friction rises, and projects begin to tailspin.

Pro Tip 18:

> Consider adopting a decision-making framework to resolve role ambiguity.

Conflicting Objectives

Defects, backlog, and technical debt, oh my!

In every project, there is always a tug-of-war between "business" and "technical" factions that we can summarize as follows.

> In the next release, how many new features do we include, and how many known problems (bugs and technical debt) do we fix?

Obviously, the "business" wants more features, while the "technocrats" are concerned with the system's long-term structural viability.

What's a Project Manager to do?

Confession 39:

> Many Project Managers fail to weather the tsunami of "critical" features demanded by checkbook-wielding stakeholders.

Like petulant children refusing to swallow some foul-tasting medicine, many stakeholders are not technically savvy enough to understand what's important for their systems. Thus, if PMs allow laypersons to run roughshod over the professionals, the structural foundation of the resulting system will suffer.

I'm sorry, but it's true.

When this occurs, projects fail, and ultimately everyone pays—most notably the users.

Pro Tip 19:

> Before project kickoff, negotiate a percentage of velocity reserved for the technical team to address bugs and technical debt in every sprint or development cycle.

It's not a perfect solution, but it goes a long way to addressing the needs of both communities.

The Business Analyst

In many organizations, internal policies and politics prohibit programmers from meeting directly with users. In such cases, technical staff must work with Business Analysts (BAs) who (ostensibly) represent the users and their needs.

The upside of this approach is that Business Analysts are allegedly proficient at expressing user requirements in technical terms. The downside is that this project structure rarely succeeds because Business Analysts often lack the necessary skills to accomplish this task.

Confession 40:

> The Business Analyst may be the most significant single point of failure in any IT project.

Unfortunately, Business Analysts don't always understand the business as well as the users they purport to represent, and they are often unfamiliar with the technology used to build modern systems. Thus, in practice, this added layer of indirection (dare I say, misdirection?) often leads to confusion and friction among users and development staff.

Pro Tip 20:

> Allows development teams to interact with user communities.

There's no need for a middle person. Developers can wear nice shirts and understand how to comport themselves professionally in front of users and customers (i.e., "the suits").

Egos

To some degree, everyone's ego affects their self-esteem, and for many folks, it's why they spring out of bed every morning and sprint to work. Indeed, many projects would run out of steam without the engine of someone's ego.

However, upon reflection, you might also realize that individual ego directly conflicts with the concept of teamwork.

Confession 41:

> Many Project Managers, Architects, and Technical Leads allow their egos to affect team morale, system quality, and project success.

Leaders at every level must balance their desire to singlehandedly push the ball over the goal line and allow other team members to handle the ball now and then.

Controlling Expectations

When you watch a romcom,[12] you expect the romantic leads to find a way to overcome every obstacle, fall in love, and eventually live happily ever after. If the movie doesn't end that way, the story's climax better be excellent; otherwise, viewers will likely be greatly disappointed.

The same holds for IT projects: Every stakeholder wants to "fall in love" with their new system. But for that to happen, it better meet their expectations.

Confession 42:

Most Project Managers undervalue the importance of managing stakeholder expectations.

The *raison d'être* of all software applications—indeed all IT systems in general—is to solve problems. The only way to know if they succeed in that goal is to have a clearly defined set of objectives established *a priori*.

Clearly, if everyone agrees on the objectives, then determining the success or failure of a given project is simple. However, if stakeholders don't share identical expectations, the conclusions will vary with the beholder.

Indeed, many projects "fail" simply because they never established formal metrics of success.

Pro Tip 21:

Under sell and overdeliver.

Never promise more than you believe your team can reasonably deliver. Otherwise, update your resume because the repercussions of unrealized promises can have broad consequences.

---

12 This term is shorthand for "romantic comedy."

Lacking Objectivity

If you were a high school music teacher, you'd likely consider your student orchestra's abilities when selecting pieces for them to play. Similarly, project leadership should objectively assess their team's effectiveness— experience, skillsets, and talents—when developing schedules, designing systems, and selecting technologies.

Confession 43:

> Project leadership often fails to assess a team's capabilities objectively.

Don't fail to take into account your organization's (lack of) capabilities. If you don't, you might set your project up to fail or, what might be worse, sell your team short.

SUMMARY

Projects fail for many reasons. Indeed, when you reflect on everything that can possibly go wrong, it's a wonder that any succeed.

Project success requires that many individual parts function as a cohesive whole. Therefore, team leaders must find ways to overcome myriad obstacles in their quest to achieve that elusive goal: Stakeholder happiness.

9

What Is the Future Role of the Enterprise Architect?

Life can only be understood backwards, but it must be lived forwards.

—*Søren Kierkegaard*

The future depends on what you do today.

—*Mahatma Gandhi*

INTRODUCTION

To paraphrase the Charles Dickens character, Oliver Twist:

Question:	"What do you want from technology?"
Answer:	"Please, sir, I want some more."

Users, consumers—human beings in general—all share one attribute: They want newer, cheaper, better, faster—and lots more of it. Indeed, one of the main, albeit unspoken, responsibilities of Enterprise Architects is to satisfy that demand.

That raises the question: How?

DOI: 10.1201/9781003414285-9

In broad strokes, we can answer that question as follows:

- Continue the digital transformation
- Automate *everything*
- Integrate new technologies into existing solutions

Although correct, that answer is incomplete because the Enterprise Architect's role must also change. In the sections below, we will present and discuss how EA's responsibilities will expand and adapt to meet the challenges of this century.

ENHANCED RESPONSIBILITIES

As I've suggested throughout this book, professional Enterprise Architects have responsibilities far beyond the technical domain. They must also serve as counselors, coaches, and consciences. In addition, they must act as custodians and curators for organizations' most significant investments: Digital resources.

But, as we'll see, it doesn't end there. If the role of Enterprise Architect is to persist, the individuals serving in that capacity must continue to add value.

Risk Management

Enterprise Architects must become increasingly familiar with risk management. As budgets and investments in IT grow, EAs must participate in identifying, assessing, and managing an organization's financial, security, and legal liabilities.

Such safeguards are increasingly becoming integral to the designs, topologies, methodologies, and infrastructures that form the foundation of an organization's IT investment.

Organizational Strategist

Technology is not just responsive—it also drives change.

Enterprise Architects must identify innovations while they're still on the horizon to anticipate their potential impacts, assess their benefits, and develop integration plans long before the tide makes them available to those waiting on shore.

EAs can then leverage that analysis to help guide their organization's long-term direction and strategy.

Culture

The culture of the modern workforce continues to change, reflecting the shifting attitudes of the labor pool. Increasingly, work/career is no longer the first or second most important priority for today's professionals.

This employment evolution affects how Enterprise Architects address many aspects of IT development, including:

- Motivating technical personnel
- Managing stakeholder expectations
- Negotiating change
- Structuring teams

It matters not whether you think this change in mindset is beneficial. It's here to stay, so as an EA, you must accept it and address it.

Sitting at the Big Table

In many extended families—mine included—holiday gatherings were so large that there was always a separate "kiddie table" where the children found themselves relegated to eat dinner. As you approached the age of majority, you longed for the day you received the invitation to sit with the grown-ups at the "big table."

That's how it often feels being an Enterprise Architect. The adults (i.e., the C-level executives) sit at the "big conference" table while the EAs wait patiently for directives and fiats to appear in their inboxes.

That's changing, however.

Increasingly, organizations are establishing the role of Chief Enterprise Architect (CEA), who, like other C-level executives, may now sit at the "big table." Allowing the CEA to sit with the "adults" is noteworthy for several reasons, including:

- It underscores the significance of IT investments
- It highlights the importance of the CEA's role
- CEAs may now contribute to and influence an organization's strategic planning

Of course, there are no exceptions to the "no free lunches" rule. Thus, this newfound power in the guise of prestige and influence comes with a price. CEAs can no longer remain myopically focused on technology as a tactical anodyne. On the contrary, more than ever, CEAs must view IT solutions as just another weapon in an organization's arsenal and find ways to aim its power in ways that advance strategic goals.

Many EAs might find this a profound change in focus.

ENHANCED DIRECTIONS

As technology continues driving solutions, Enterprise Architects will need to navigate the following course changes.

The Cloud

Enterprise Architects should plan migrations to cloud-based solutions for organizations that can benefit from such designs. However, despite all the hype you might have heard, this is not as easy as the cloud vendors' advertising might have you believe.

Shocking, I know.

Most organizations cannot afford to shut down operations while a "cloud transformation" occurs. Thus, EAs must develop strategies that, in effect, support changing an aircraft's wings while it's in flight. In other words, the EA must develop a migration strategy that does not negatively impact day-to-day operations.

This is not a simple task.

Moreover, cloud computing may not be suitable for every organization. Indeed, many IT shops might benefit from a hybrid solution: Retain support for mission-critical applications in-house while migrating all ancillary systems to the cloud.

Avoid Accidental Architecture

As enterprise architecture becomes increasingly significant, Enterprise Architects can't leave it to chance. It's just too risky.

Thus, EAs must develop a "future path" that includes

- An accurate assessment of the "as is" architecture
- A robust design of the "to be" architecture
- A fully developed transition plan

Focus on the Value Proposition

Contrary to widespread belief, technology is not a toy but a tool. Thus, regardless of the domain—IT, medicine, housing, etc.—it only has value when it *benefits* an organization or its user community.

Thus, Enterprise Architects—indeed everyone working in IT—must ensure that every technical decision, product selection, and design choice delivers *value* to the organization, its users, and its customers.

Understand that technology is the tail, not the dog. For many EAs and IT shops, this is a radical change in focus.

Infrastructure Rules

Whether in-house, cloud-based, or a hybrid design, a sizable percentage of an organization's technology investment is in its infrastructure.

Like a house, the soundness of an IT architecture begins with its foundation. Therefore, every enterprise architecture must address security, availability, reliability, etc. The more "ilities" the infrastructure provides, the fewer each application must deliver individually.

Stated another way, when features are integral to the infrastructure, you must only get them right *once*. Otherwise, every application must implement them correctly—and consistently—every time.

Thus, regardless of its location (in-house or remote), Enterprise Architects should design the infrastructure so application developers can view it as if it were an Infrastructure as a Service (IaaS), Platform as a Service (PaaS), or Software as a Service (SaaS) offering. If done correctly, there is immense potential to achieve economies of scale.

EAs should not squander this opportunity.

Full Lifecycle Support

As a new-age Enterprise Architect, your job no longer ends when the release manager presses the "deploy" button. Indeed, in some sense, it's just beginning.

Some of an EA's post-deployment responsibilities include:

- Monitoring system performance
- Assessing bug reports
- Reviewing operational issues
- Observing the impacts on the help desk support personnel

The information you glean during this phase should serve as a feedback loop. Improvements to any shortcomings you identify should find their way into subsequent releases and future designs.

ENHANCED OBJECTIVES

Enterprise Architects can no longer remain "one-trick ponies," focusing on a limited set of technologies and methodologies. Indeed, as described below, EAs must integrate all the following objectives into their practices.

Data Drives Design

You are probably familiar with James Carville's 1992 quote, "It's the economy, stupid." Indeed, sound advice for any politician in any era.

However, in the information-driven world of IT, we need to revise the quote to read, "It's the data, stupid."

Data are the keys to every organization's dominion and survival. It can no longer be an afterthought. Instead, data should reside at the hub of every organization's wheel, supporting every spoke at every turn. Therefore, Enterprise Architects need to analyze, categorize, prioritize, organize, and utilize data in ways that underscore its importance.

AI Enhanced Design

Undoubtedly, there is an immense amount of hype surrounding the power and scope of Artificial Intelligence (AI). Surprisingly, however, much of the hyperbole is true.

Enterprise Architects can no longer treat AI as a fringe technology useful in limited applications such as image recognition and natural language processing. On the contrary, AI has become mainstream and thus should move closer to center stage in modern system design.

Security Rules

In my experience, the main objective of every cyber security expert is to develop unique ways to repeat a mantra like "no" when reviewing new designs. Mind you, they never tell you what you *should do*. On the contrary, they just say "no" to anything you propose doing.

Thus, the onus usually falls on the Enterprise Architect's shoulder to develop designs incorporating adequate security measures.

This responsibility has only grown in recent years as the profitability and sophistication of hacking have increased. Thus, all EAs must become experts in security technology, and it should become a primary consideration in all designs and every product selection.

Digital Transformation

Digital Transformation (DT) is no longer a buzzword. Instead, it's become both a driver and a destination because it transforms the processes, culture, and user interaction. It reimagines organizations and the way they engage and interact with customers.

Enterprise Architects should ensure that every modernization effort focuses on DT. However, although DT seems technology-driven, it's NOT just an IT initiative. Because it transforms organizations, DT is an all-hands effort.

SUMMARY

Although many folks don't realize it, the age-old expression, "May you live in interesting times," is a curse, not a blessing. The idea is that during dull periods, life is much easier and far more enjoyable.

I guess that may be a matter of opinion.

However, fortunately or unfortunately, the IT industry finds itself hurtling headlong into interesting times due to the advancement and rapid development of new technologies. Thus, the demand for professional and implacable Enterprise Architects will only increase. Moreover, their roles and relative significance within organizations will expand commensurately.

That said, the job is not for everyone. Nor is everyone qualified to do it.

Nevertheless, for individuals possessing the desire, talent, and temerity to tackle it, the personal and professional rewards are, in my opinion, well worth the sacrifices.

But that's just one person's opinion.

Since this has been my rant, we'll leave it at that.

Appendix

THE PLAYERS

I'll take actors and their roles for one hundred, Alex.

—*Anonymous*

Actors / Roles	Description
Actors	When modeling IT systems, Actors represent users, systems, or events (such as time-based triggers) that interact with an application.
Business Analysts	A Business Analyst is an individual who analyzes the processes and procedures of an organization to identify and rectify operational issues. (See *Peter Principle* in the Glossary.)
CEA	A Chief Enterprise Architect (CEA) is responsible for developing, maintaining, and extending an organization's IT investment.
CIO	A Chief Information Officer (CIO) is the executive responsible for the management, development, and usability of all information and computer technologies within an organization.
Clients	A Client is an individual or organization to which professionals render their services. See also, *Stakeholder*.
Consumers	An Actor that receives and processes *events*. Actors can assume many forms, such as Users (see below) or other systems.
CTO	A Chief Technology Officer (CTO) is the executive responsible for addressing an organization's technological requirements, which often include its R&D efforts.
Customers	A Customer is an individual or an organization that acquires goods and services from.
DBA	Database Administrator.
Developers	See *Software Developer*.
Enterprise Architects	An Enterprise Architect is responsible for planning, developing, implementing, and maintaining an organization's investment in Information Technology.

Actors / Roles	Description
Portfolio Managers	Portfolio Managers oversee an organization's IT investment. They ensure that tactical initiatives align with strategic goals, develop future objectives, and manage one or more ongoing programs.
Producers	A Producer is an Actor that generates *events*.
Program Manager	Based on the portfolio's objectives, a Program Manager prioritizes projects, monitors budgets, resolves resource contention among competing initiatives, and, most importantly, manages risk.
Programmer	A Programmer is an IT professional whose primary responsibility is writing code (i.e., *software*). See also, *Software Developer* and *Software Engineer*.
Project Lead	A Project Lead assumes the same roles and responsibilities as a Project Manager for a subset of a project. For example, there are often Project Leads for the UI, the Controller, the data layer, etc.
Project Manager	A Project Manager's responsibilities are akin to that of a Program Manager but at the project level: They plan, budget, oversee, and manage risk for individual projects.
Release Manager	The engineer responsible for deploying systems.
SME	Subject Matter Expert.
Software Developers	Software Developers typically have a broader scope than Programmers. Their responsibilities usually extend to the entire SDLC. See also, *Programmer* and *Software Engineer*.
Software Engineers	Although often confused with the term Software Developer, A Software Engineer designs and develops software solutions that Programmers code.
Stakeholders	A Stakeholder is an individual or organization interested in a project or enterprise.
Users	A User is an individual authorized to interact and leverage the services of an application, computer system, or network capability.

THE PRO TIPS

I always pass on good advice. It is the only thing to do with it. It is never of any use to oneself.

—*Oscar Wilde*

Chapter	Tip #	Page #	Text
2	1	13	As a rule, you should design *holistically* and develop *incrementally*.
2	2	41	When talking to the "number crunchers," emphasize that developing an Enterprise Architecture won't instantly help the bottom line.
3	1	56	An Enterprise Architect should establish a guidepost even if it has to move rather than leaving the development team directionless.
3	2	60	Instead of railing about issues, Enterprise Architects should try to find technical solutions to project management challenges.
3	3	65	Start a design with some simple components. Then, you can extend, modify, and correct that early draft as needed.
3	4	66	Don't assume anything; verify everything.
3	5	66	Like voting in many congressional districts, Enterprise Architects should request design feedback early and often.
3	6	68	Enterprise Architects should use the "back channel" judiciously but without reservation if it's available.
3	7	71	Delay compromise as long as possible.
3	8	73	EAs should include ROI and CBA analyses as part of the business plan for any reasonably sized projects.
3	9	75	Follow the Rule of Three.
4	1	84	Enterprise Architects should not limit their focus to technology.

Chapter	Tip #	Page #	Text
4	2	86	Using maps, methodologies, recipes, instruction booklets, rules-of-thumb, hunches, etc., guides our efforts toward a goal, but they don't preclude the need to think. Don't just assume that blindly following the adopted methodology will lead you to the best solution. Take time to understand the consequences of a choice before selecting it.
4	3	89	It's better to start with a plan—even if (when!) it changes—than simply taking off and gliding with the wind.
4	4	94	Given the extraordinary benefits at such modest costs, architects and designers should consider wrapping every external component.
5	1	106	Adding and combining components in a design should be a deliberate action based on a sound rationale, adding value to the overall solution.
5	2	106	The least expensive and most reliable component is the one that is never built or deployed.
5	3	107	Designers should "shoot for the stars" before "returning to Earth."
5	4	111	All system parameters should be externalized and reside in a central store available to all system components.
5	5	112	Screens should "construct" themselves upon invocation based on the user's role.
5	6	112	The build process should generate inter-process message formats.
5	7	112	Design guidelines should eliminate (or severely restrict) the use of manifest constants in programs.
5	8	112	Most database attributes should be of type VARCHAR—even numeric fields.
5	9	118	Simplify, simplify, simplify.
6	1	124	Outside consultants who serve as Enterprise Architects should test the waters before making waves.
6	2	131	If you hit a process speed bump or determine a formalism doesn't integrate well into your organization's culture, change it, or avoid it.
6	3	131	Hire the best team you can, point them in the right direction, then get out of their way.

Chapter	Tip #	Page #	Text
6	4	132	When re-estimating, don't go back to the well more than once. If you need to slip your schedule by one month, ask for three (or six!). You'll receive the same beating, but you'll have gained enough "runway" to complete the project comfortably without sacrificing quality (and will have obtained enough time to let the wounds heal).
6	5	135	Let your leaders lead.
6	6	136	People skills count: find ways to use and hone them.
6	7	137	When dealing with challenging personalities, make it appear that every decision is the stakeholder's idea.
6	8	138	Don't sell features. Sell benefits.
6	9	140	Employ the Rule of Three.
6	10	140	If you want to have any clients tomorrow, take care of your customers today.
6	11	142	Examine your work product first.
6	12	148	Know your destination.
6	13	149	Assemble the best team you can.
6	14	149	Requirements Rule!
6	15	150	Deliver value with each release.
6	16	150	Enterprise Architects should design for a marathon, not a sprint.
6	17	151	Conduct design reviews regularly.
6	18	151	Software Engineering Rules!
6	19	152	Nail down the system's infrastructure.
6	20	152	Instrumentation Rules!
6	21	153	Never sacrifice quality.
6	22	153	Set the bar high.
6	23	154	Don't defer Technical Debt and bug remediation.
6	24	154	Testing Rules!
6	25	155	Users Rule!
6	26	155	Documentation Rules!
6	27	155	The "ilities" can't be an afterthought
7	1	177	Be responsive.
7	2	177	Don't engage in handwaves.
7	3	177	Provide realistic schedules.
7	4	178	If the schedule slips, wear it.

Chapter	Tip #	Page #	Text
7	5	178	Ask for more time than you need.
7	6	179	Delay significant decisions for as long as you can.
7	7	179	Own up to your mistakes.
7	8	180	Explicitly determine during the early stages of a project which of the four fundamental project attributes—cost, performance, functionality, and schedule—are most important to your stakeholders.
7	9	180	Track backlog and technical debt closely because they are early warning indicators of widespread project issues.
7	10	181	Always remain professional.
7	11	181	Address bugs as they arise.
7	12	181	Never forget that politics rule.
7	13	182	Verify everything—personally.
7	14	182	Project sponsors who manage the IT budgets hold more power than you might otherwise imagine.
7	15	183	Do your homework.
7	16	183	Don't rely on Project Managers.
7	17	183	Don't let the pursuit of perfection become the nemesis of realizing excellence.
7	18	184	Take small bites of the apple.
7	19	184	Stay current.
7	20	185	Support test teams.
7	21	185	Always walk the cat backward.
7	22	185	You never have time for shortcuts.
7	23	185	If you don't know, say so.
7	24	186	Keep your word.
7	25	186	If you're an independent contractor, never say "no."
7	26	186	Stay calm.
7	27	187	Don't be autocratic.
8	1	194	Take time to *think*.
8	2	196	Include the technology team during the project formulation stage.
8	3	197	Enterprise Architects should avoid politics to the extent possible. But when forced to engage, they should do so impartially, espousing what's best for the organization in the large, not an individual fiefdom.

Chapter	Tip #	Page #	Text
8	4	198	Include the technical team when performing feature triage because they can often group requirements in ways that allow the best bang for the limited development dollar.
8	5	199	Validate every decision based on how it affects every class of user.
8	6	201	Develop a formal Business Architecture and disseminate it to all project team members.
8	7	203	Trust, but verify.
8	8	204	Review requirements and system specifications carefully.
8	9	207	To restrain scope creep, develop strong technical and financial arguments that clearly articulate their impact.
8	10	207	Planners should plan.
8	11	208	Enterprise Architects should ensure every technical and project decision has the user in mind.
8	12	216	Resist the urge to increase team size when mitigating schedule delays.
8	13	217	Try to right-size your projects.
8	14	218	Don't waste developer time.
8	15	220	When identified, replace deadwood with mighty oaks or some sturdy saplings whenever possible.
8	16	225	I recommend not using a new product or a new version of an existing product until it has sufficient flight time to ensure that it flies smoothly. Instead, let beta testers and early adopters serve as test pilots.
8	17	226	Never rely on products offered by startups unless the company is willing to place its source code in escrow and make it available to customers in the event of their demise.
8	18	228	Consider adopting a decision-making framework to resolve role ambiguity.
8	19	229	Before project kickoff, negotiate a percentage of velocity reserved for the technical team to address bugs and technical debt in every sprint or development cycle.
8	20	230	Allows development teams to interact with user communities.
8	21	231	Under sell and overdeliver.

THE CONFESSIONS

Confession is good for the soul.

—*Scottish proverb*

Chapter	Confession #	Page #	Confession Text
1	1	6	Anyone can call themselves an Architect.
1	2	6	Anyone can call themselves an Enterprise Architect.
1	3	7	Even the best Enterprise Architects are NOT always right.
2	1	13	Many Enterprise Architects don't address their organization's long-term needs when designing solutions.
2	2	13	Like many Enterprise Architects, some stakeholders don't want to address their organization's long-term IT needs.
2	3	14	You never have enough time for shortcuts.
2	4	22	Many Enterprise Architects don't consider quality attributes during the design phase.
2	5	22	Enterprise Architects don't have the luxury of ignoring the "boring" or "trivial" aspects of a system or its design.
2	6	29	Despite what some architects profess, the newest technology is not necessarily the best choice.
2	7	30	Many application architects feel they must "strut their stuff" by including the "latest and greatest" technologies in their designs.
2	8	37	Security Architects are delighted to tell you what you *shouldn't* do but rarely instruct you on what you *should* do.
2	9	37	Application Architects are wont to gripe ad nauseam about adopting a cookie-cutter approach to design and the lack of forethought and missed opportunities when stakeholders reject the inclusion of new technologies.

Chapter	Confession #	Page #	Confession Text
2	10	42	Enterprise Architecture is about *change*.
2	11	42	Accommodating change is the sole constant in the professional life of an Enterprise Architect.
2	12	42	Enterprise Architecture must enable interoperability and extension.
2	13	43	System performance is often an afterthought for many Enterprise Architects.
2	14	43	Many Enterprise Architects forget that data is the most valuable asset of any organization.
2	15	44	Many IT designers—not just architects—forget that simplicity counts.
3	1	48	Many architectural roles are not fully understood by stakeholders (or other architects, for that matter).
3	2	51	Many Enterprise Architects cannot cope with the vortex of confusion synonymous with system development.
3	3	51	Regardless of culpability, Enterprise Architects serve as the lightning rod for every "bolt from the blue."
3	4	52	Many Enterprise Architects actively avoid difficult decisions.
3	5	53	Many Enterprise Architects are one-trick ponies.
3	6	54	Many Enterprise Architects don't have the self-confidence to admit when they lack pertinent expertise.
3	7	55	A professional Enterprise Architect learns on the job.
3	8	55	In addition to being One-Trick Ponies, many Enterprise Architects are lazy.
3	9	56	Many Enterprise Architects lack common sense.
3	10	56	Many Enterprise Architects lack the capacity, disposition, desire, or determination to establish a technological vision.
3	11	57	You would be dismayed to discover how many Enterprise Architects lack this skill.

Chapter	Confession #	Page #	Confession Text
3	12	57	Many Enterprise Architects give short shrift to an organization's Transition Plan.
3	13	58	Many Enterprise Architects believe they need not concern themselves with such mundane considerations as an organization's goals and vision.
3	14	58	Many Enterprise Architects have one favorite architectural model they will employ regarding its efficacy in a given situation.
3	15	59	Many Enterprise Architects view hardware as a necessary evil.
3	16	59	Many Enterprise Architects do not address security concerns until late in the SDLC.
3	17	61	Many Enterprise Architects don't believe mentoring is part of their responsibilities.
3	18	62	Many Enterprise Architects are poor communicators.
3	19	62	Many Enterprise Architects don't like to engage with stakeholders.
3	20	63	Many Enterprise Architects simply want to tread water and float with the tide.
3	21	64	Many Enterprise Architects have a "fire and forget" attitude.
3	22	65	Many Enterprise Architects have difficulty overcoming personal inertia when designing in a greenfield.
3	23	67	Not all Enterprise Architects welcome feedback.
3	24	67	Ingenuity doesn't work on a clock.
3	25	68	Many Enterprise Architects too often rely on "cozy solutions."
3	26	69	The title "Enterprise Architect" should not be conferred based on a popularity contest.
3	27	69	Many Enterprise Architects don't realize (or choose to ignore the fact) that it's the users who'll bear the brunt of bad architecture.
3	28	70	Some Enterprise Architects compromise too early.

Chapter	Confession #	Page #	Confession Text
3	29	72	Most Enterprise Architects don't educate senior stakeholders about the costs and benefits of IT investment.
3	30	73	Many Enterprise Architects don't understand how to compute or leverage the benefits of an ROI or CBA analysis.
3	31	74	Many Enterprise Architects hold their clients in disdain.
3	32	75	Many Enterprise Architects shade the truth in such a way as to engineer decisions.
3	33	76	Few Enterprise Architects admit to mistakes.
3	34	76	Many Enterprise Architects are self-important, self-proclaimed demigods.
3	35	76	Many Enterprise Architects act like "lone wolves."
3	36	77	Not every Enterprise Architect is a dedicated, hard-working professional.
3	37	78	Many stakeholders believe an Enterprise Architect is merely a senior developer with a fancy appellation.
3	38	78	Many organizations believe that good developers make good Enterprise Architects.
3	39	78	Many IT professionals—especially software developers—believe that Enterprise Architects are "technical has-beens."
4	1	82	Many Enterprise Architects don't appreciate that Enterprise Architecture is not just about components.
4	2	82	Many Enterprise Architects don't formalize component integration.
4	3	83	Many Enterprise Architects don't appreciate the significance of their decisions.
4	4	84	Many Enterprise Architects don't appreciate that their decisions not only affect system design but also impact the development environment and influence the structure of project teams.
4	5	85	Many Enterprise Architects are one-trick ponies.

Chapter	Confession #	Page #	Confession Text
4	6	86	Many Enterprise Architects rely on methodology to avoid architecture.
4	7	87	Architecture on the fly doesn't work.
4	8	87	Most Enterprise Architects—indeed most project stakeholders—don't understand the impact of Technical Debt.
4	9	89	Many Enterprise Architects are not savvy enough to appreciate the scope and extent of the artifacts required for a given project.
4	10	90	Architects, Project Managers, and Technical Leads don't leverage Just-in-Time (JIT) development practices.
4	11	92	Many Enterprise Architects suffer from the NIH Syndrome.
4	12	94	Many IT professionals—not just Enterprise Architects—undervalue the benefits of developing Wrapper Functions.
4	13	95	There is often a lack of shared focus among the disparate architectural disciplines within an organization.
4	14	95	Most Enterprise Architects are unaware of the importance of adopting a holistic view.
4	15	96	You can't judge the quality of a design in a vacuum.
4	16	97	Many Enterprise Architects attribute too much design importance to meeting functional requirements.
4	17	97	Most Enterprise Architects give short shrift to the "ilities."
4	18	97	It's often difficult to isolate "ilities."
4	19	98	Many system architects—software designers in general—create unwieldy components.
4	20	98	Many architects and software designers often don't design for reusability.
4	21	98	Many architects are unaware that a solid design allows for the independent development of components.

Chapter	Confession #	Page #	Confession Text
4	22	98	Many Enterprise Architects don't identify critical use cases and use them to vet their designs.
4	23	99	If an Enterprise Architect does not feel comfortable generating estimates from a proposed architecture, the design requires additional refinement.
4	24	99	Many architects miss the fact that their designs contain God Objects.
4	25	99	Many Enterprise Architects don't realize they can become victims of their own success.
4	26	100	Most development teams don't adequately document designs.
5	1	102	It comes as a surprise to many software engineers that, by definition, architecture creates design problems.
5	2	103	There isn't a clear demarcation indicating where architecture ends, and design begins.
5	3	105	Many Enterprise Architects and Software Designers don't realize that their goal is to create a solution wherein the whole is greater than the sum of the parts.
5	4	106	When stuck, many Enterprise Architects and System Designers simply "draw another box."
	5	107	Many architects and designers compromise too early.
5	6	108	Many architects and designers succumb to the NIH Syndrome.
5	7	109	Many architects lack formal training in the methods, procedures, and theories of system design.
5	8	110	Many designers ignore the benefits of Stepwise Refinement.
	9	110	Many designers are unfamiliar with the KISS principle.
5	10	111	Many Architects have never crossed paths with an assumption they wouldn't readily integrate into their designs.

Chapter	Confession #	Page #	Confession Text
5	11	111	Many Architects are not opposed to hardcoding their assumptions.
5	12	113	Too many architects fall so in love with their designs that they cannot "throw in the towel" when "boxed into a corner."
5	13	113	Handwaving is the most common form of physical exercise for many architects and designers.
5	14	114	Novice architects often begin coding before completing a design.
5	15	114	For many designers, instrumentation is often an afterthought.
5	16	114	Most architects don't even consider testability.
5	17	115	Most Project Stakeholders don't appreciate the importance of Requirements Traceability as part of the SDLC.
5	18	115	You never have enough time for shortcuts.
5	19	116	Designers need more technical depth than Architects.
5	20	116	The Resume Factor is far more prevalent than most stakeholders would believe.
5	21	117	Architects overlook the importance of aesthetics in a design.
5	22	117	Most designers don't know when to stop.
5	23	118	Most designers don't appreciate the ramifications of their efforts.
6	1	123	Most Enterprise Architects don't consider the implications of a project's composition.
6	2	124	Many Enterprise Architects don't consider their role within the sponsoring organization.
6	3	125	Most organizations don't spend enough time gathering and organizing preliminary requirements.
6	4	125	In many cases, initial project estimates are so inaccurate that approvers would be better off developing their own assessments.

Chapter	Confession #	Page #	Confession Text
6	5	126	Most organizations develop their initial project estimates without involving the Enterprise Architect and senior designers.
6	6	126	Project sponsors want to avoid sticker shock.
6	7	128	Most Project Managers and Enterprise Architects don't consider the project costs and risks when determining the extent of the initial architectural effort.
6	8	129	Enterprise Architects often manage stakeholder expectations by promoting short-term gains and avoiding any discussion of long-term disadvantages a particular design approach might impose on a project.
6	9	130	Methodologies are no substitute for thinking.
6	10	130	Methodologies don't ensure success.
6	11	131	Methodologies can "get in the way" of success.
6	12	131	Methodology is no substitute for talent.
6	13	131	Talent will succeed in the absence of methodology.
6	14	132	You rarely have time for shortcuts.
6	15	133	In many organizations, the demarcation of duties blurs among Portfolio, Program, and Project managers.
6	16	134	Many IT development shops lack Project Leaders.
6	17	135	Leadership is not commonplace, not conferred by title, and doesn't come conveniently packaged as a gel in a squeeze tube positioned next to the gum, chocolate bars, and energy drinks on shelves found along the checkout aisles in supermarkets.
6	18	136	IT consulting is an excellent profession—if we could only eliminate the human element.
6	19	137	Fighting with stakeholders is self-defeating—even when you're right.

Chapter	Confession #	Page #	Confession Text
6	20	139	One of the essential tasks of an Enterprise Architect is educating stakeholders, clients, and users.
6	21	139	Not all seemingly irrational stakeholder decisions are mistakes.
6	22	140	Most stakeholders can sniff out insincerity.
6	23	141	Many Enterprise Architects take the easy way out and design the same systems repeatedly.
6	24	142	Due to inexperience, apprehension, or fecklessness, many Enterprise Architects opt to deflect rather than assume responsibility for issues.
6	25	143	While mired in the vortex of confusion, many Enterprise Architects miss the means of escape: Efficiency.
6	26	143	Many Enterprise Architects incorporate technologies solely to fill holes in their resumes.
6	27	144	Many Enterprise Architects expend little effort to remain current with technology.
6	28	144	Most IT shops develop some degree of dysfunction.
6	29	145	Many project teams suffer from poor leadership.
6	30	145	Many team leaders loathe making decisions.
6	31	146	Many teams lack peer accountability.
6	32	146	Politeness counts!
6	33	147	Often, some team members lack the desire and willingness to communicate.
6	34	147	Some team members simply don't like one another.
6	35	151	Many Enterprise Architects don't concern themselves with long-term issues because they don't plan to be with the project long-term.
6	36	152	Ingenuity doesn't work on a schedule.

Chapter	Confession #	Page #	Confession Text
7	1	159	Complexity Reduction remains overlooked by many modern IT designers who seem compelled to include every artifice and technique they know in every architecture they develop, regardless of its benefits to the project or the organization.
7	2	159	Many organizations don't track the costs and expenses associated with ongoing system maintenance. Instead, they form a "software engineering team" and squeeze as many modifications and extensions as they can into its budget.
7	3	160	Many organizations allow individual development teams to make "one-off" decisions regarding technology and componentry.
7	4	160	Many organizations adopt a policy that allows new technology to deploy with new systems, which can often undermine the stability of the enterprise infrastructure.
7	5	161	Many Enterprise Architects conceal architectural design deficiencies using a straightforward and popular estimating technique called a SWAG.
7	6	162	Because many believe knowledge is power, information sharing occurs only begrudgingly in some organizations.
7	7	163	Many Enterprise Architects cannot create helpful abstractions that they can employ to convey complex ideas to non-technical staff.
7	8	163	Many Enterprise Architects tend to shoehorn tomorrow's problems into yesterday's solutions.
7	9	164	Many Enterprise Architects capitulate at the first signs of resistance.
7	10	164	Many Enterprise Architects become disgruntled when decisions don't align with their recommendations.
7	11	165	Many Enterprise Architects lose their way at the first unexpected crossroads.
7	12	166	Deciding whether to share "back channel" information is often difficult.

Chapter	Confession #	Page #	Confession Text
7	13	166	Because of the elevated ethical expectations, many Enterprise Architects believe they can't—or shouldn't—expose their mistakes.
7	14	167	Many Enterprise Architects address symptoms, not causes.
7	15	168	Many Enterprise Architects refuse to accept the practical realities of a given situation.
7	16	168	Many Enterprise Architects adhere to the ultimatum, "It's either my way or the highway."
7	17	169	Many stakeholders use email to "paint" a "customized" record of "reality."
7	18	170	Meetings are a necessary evil.
7	19	171	Many Enterprise Architects suffer from "cubism."
7	20	171	Enterprise architects do most of their work in "real-time."
8	1	192	Many projects are poorly scoped.
8	2	193	Many projects are poorly designed.
8	3	195	For many projects, deadlines are artificial.
8	4	196	Politics is not the sole province of government or C-Level executives.
8	5	197	As the old saying goes, if everything is a priority, then nothing is a priority.
8	6	198	In many project teams, the user is the last consideration.
8	7	198	Many stakeholders don't realize there are many classes of users.
8	8	200	User indifference engenders lackluster applications that create more problems than they solve.
8	9	200	Withholding knowledge is the sine qua non for most organizations.
8	10	200	Many organizations treat development staff like mushrooms: They're kept in the dark, covered in manure.
8	11	201	Many organizations are unaware of the benefits of developing a Business Architecture.

Chapter	Confession #	Page #	Confession Text
8	12	202	Most organizational subdivisions suffer from the NIH Syndrome: They firmly believe that if they didn't build it, it isn't any good, and they shouldn't use it.
8	13	203	Errors of omission are far more prevalent and pernicious than most senior executives would imagine.
8	14	204	Vague requirements are shockingly prevalent and are a significant cause of project failure.
8	15	206	Because it typically originates with checkbook-wielding stakeholders, scope creep often goes unchallenged.
8	16	207	Many project planners prioritize features "on the fly."
8	17	208	In many IT shops, the "user" is only a vague concept.
8	18	208	There is never enough time for shortcuts.
8	19	209	Many organizations hide the impact of poor system design during project maintenance cycles.
8	20	211	Many organizations don't appreciate that, absent a formal enterprise architecture to cushion them from changes in the wind, even a gentle breeze will alter their route.
8	21	212	Many Enterprise Architects fail to incorporate their organization's goals into their designs.
8	22	212	Many Enterprise Architects adhere to the "fire and forget" rule.
8	23	213	Many Enterprise Architects defer consideration of the "ilities" until it's too late in the project lifecycle to mitigate any resulting issues.
8	24	213	Some Enterprise Architects don't know how to integrate the "ilities" into their designs. Thus, they can't possibly demonstrate how their approach meets or exceeds the system's non-functional requirements.

Chapter	Confession #	Page #	Confession Text
8	25	215	Most stakeholders expect development staff to overcome every unexpected event and all planning, estimating, and technological deficiencies.
8	26	215	The only thing you achieve when you add staff to floundering projects is to place additional demands on the existing team members.
8	27	216	Project managers who hoard development resources usually find that their projects collapse under their own weight.
8	28	217	Most projects convene too many meetings with too many attendees addressing too many topics resulting in too little progress.
8	29	219	Every project seems to have at least one rogue developer.
8	30	220	In IT, many project managers and technical leads lack interpersonal skills.
8	31	220	In most large-scale development projects, the stellar performers often must compensate for the productivity eclipse caused by a few dark stars.
8	32	221	The best methodologies, technologies, topologies, and any other related "ologies" you can imagine won't overcome a lack of ability.
8	33	223	Many Enterprise Architects focus on technology and fail to keep the user centered in their design crosshairs.
8	34	224	Many organizations don't provide adequate resources for their design teams to conduct satisfactory product evaluations.
8	35	225	Many Enterprise Architects believe that new is better.
8	36	226	Many organizations fail to employ adequate precautions when relying on startups.
8	37	227	Many Project Managers don't know how to say "no."
8	38	228	Many Program Managers allow too much role overlap in their project teams.

Chapter	Confession #	Page #	Confession Text
8	39	229	Many Project Managers fail to weather the tsunami of "critical" features demanded by checkbook-wielding stakeholders.
8	40	230	The Business Analyst may be the most significant single point of failure in any IT project.
8	41	230	Many Project Managers, Architects, and Technical Leads allow their egos to affect team morale, system quality, and project success.
8	42	231	Most Project Managers undervalue the importance of managing stakeholder expectations.
8	43	232	Project leadership often fails to assess a team's capabilities objectively.

GLOSSARY OF TERMS

The right words to express oneself can never be found in any dictionary.

—Marty Rubin

Term	Definition/Description
Actor	An Actor is any participant involved in the planning, building, deploying, using, and monitoring of enterprise systems.
Architecture	Architecture is the art, science, and practice focused on the design and construction of buildings.
AI	Artificial Intelligence.
BA	Business Analysts.
Business Architecture	Business Architecture defines an organization's current and future state and specifies the transition plan to achieve its goals.
CBA	Cost–Benefit Analysis.
CEA	Chief Enterprise Architect.
COTS	Commercial Off the Shelf.
CRT	Cathode-Ray Tube.
C/S	Client-Server Architecture.
Data Architecture	Data Architecture defines the structure, tools, and standards that govern enterprise data collection, organization, and availability.
DBMS	Database Management System.
DDD	Domain-Driven Design.
DSS	Decision Support Systems.
DT	Digital Transformation.
EA	See *Enterprise Architect*.
Enterprise Architect	An Enterprise Architect is an expert who works with key stakeholders to develop a strategy to manage an organization's IT infrastructure, investments, and assets.
Enterprise Architecture	Enterprise Architecture is a holistic blueprint under which stakeholders can plan, govern, design, build, and deploy solutions in a cohesive manner that meets and furthers an organization's goals.
Event	Often distributed as a message, an event represents a change in the state of a system.
FL	Fuzzy Logic.
FS	Fuzzy Sets.

Term	Definition/Description
Gall's Law	A complex system that works is invariably found to have evolved from a simple system that worked. The inverse proposition also appears to be true: A complex system designed from scratch never works and cannot be made to work. You have to start over, beginning with a working simple system.
Greenfield	The term greenfield began in the construction industry. It refers to any construction site without any existing buildings on it. Thus, there is no need to raze any existing structures to make way for the new ones. In IT, the term refers to any new projects that are not replacing or integrating with any current systems.
GUI	Graphical User Interface.
Infrastructure Architecture	Infrastructure Architecture specifies low-level hardware components' structure, organization, and design.
IT	Information Technology.
IT Architecture	IT Architecture is a formal set of principles, guidelines, and diagrams that govern the design, development, and integration of components and resources.
JIT	Just-in-Time Development.
KISS Principle	Keep It Simple Stupid.
Network Effect	The Network Effect describes the circumstance where current members gain incremental benefits when new users join a group.
NIH	Not Invented Here.
NoSQL Database	NoSQL stands for "Not only SQL." It refers to databases that use non-tabular approaches to store and index data.
Occam's Razor	"Entities should not be multiplied beyond necessity."
Peter Principle	Individuals rise to "a level of respective incompetence."
PM	Project Manager.
R&D	Research and Development.
RDBMS	Relational Database Management System.
Refactoring	Refactoring is the process of revising the design and structure of source code without adding or modifying functionality.
Requirements Traceability	Requirements Traceability is the ability to trace the consequences of a requirement from its inception to its implementation.
ROI	Return on Investment.
SOA	Service-Oriented Architecture.
SDLC	Software Development Lifecycle.
SLA	Service Level Agreement.
SME	Subject Matter Expert.
Software Design	*Software Design* is the process of mapping requirements to components and ensuring that those components have the features and functionality required to implement them.

Term	Definition/Description
Technical Debt	Technical Debt refers to the accumulation of design deficiencies that render code challenging to maintain and extend, usually resulting from prioritizing schedules over quality.
The Business	This phrase is a collective term that describes Actors (typically non-technical) who perform an organization's duties *proper* rather than those Actors involved in planning and building enterprise applications.
UI	User Interface. (See also *GUI*.)
varchar	A VARCHAR is a variable character field.
WAG	Wild-ass-guess.
Wrapper Function	A *Wrapper Function* is a "thin façade" whose only task is to invoke another function after executing as little code as possible.

Index

Page numbers in *italics* indicate figures in the text

A

Accommodating change, 42
The Agony and the Ecstasy (Stone), 117
Application Architects, 29, 30, 35, 37, 38
Application architecture, 11, 19, *19*, 35–36
Architectural decisions
    architectural scope, 89–90
    code reuse design, 92–93
    component integration, 82–83
    design decision, 83–84
    development methodologies, 86
    favorite design approach, 85
    formal planning, 89
    forward-looking, 82
    holistic solutions, 94–95
    Just-in-Time (JIT) development
        practices, 90–92
    planning counts, 87
    position navigation beacons, 87
    rapid development methodology, 90, 91
    ripple effects, 84–85
    Technical Debt, 87–89
    wrapper functions, 94
Architectural metrics
    availability, 23
    elasticity, 25
    end-to-end design, 22
    extensibility, 25–26
    faulty designs, 22
    "latest and greatest" technologies, 30
    performance, 26
    quality attributes, 22
    reliability, 23–24
    scalability, 24–25
    testability, 27
Architectural views
    Application Architecture Diagram,
        19, *19*

Component Diagram, 20, *20*
Context Diagram, 19, *19*
Data Flow Diagram, 21, *21*
Deployment Diagram, 20, *20*
    example, 21, **21**
Architecture
    definition, 10
    types of, 10–11
Architecture *vs.* design, 58
    complex design example, *104*
    monolithic example, *103*
    MVC example, *103*
    SOA example, *104*
Artificial Intelligence (AI), 238–239
Availability metric, 23

B

Business Analysts (BAs), 180, 229–230
Business architecture (BA), 10–11, 33–34,
    34, 134, 201
Buyer beware mentality, 7

C

Candy factor, 116–117
Capability Model, 173
Chief Enterprise Architect (CEA),
    235, 236
C-level executives, 72, 175, 200
Client–Server (C/S) architecture, *15*, 15–16
Cloud-based solutions, 236
Code quality, 93
Component Diagram, 20, *20*
Consultants, 124, 175, 176
Context Diagram, 19, *19*
Cookie-cutter approach, 37
Cost–Benefit analysis (CBA), 72–73

D

Data architecture, 11, 34–35
Database Management Systems (DBMS), 224, 225
Data driven design, 238
Data Flow Diagram, 21, *21*
Deficient design, 193–194
Degree of professionalism, 117
Deployment Diagram, 20, *20*
Development methodologies, 60
Digital Transformation (DT), 239
Direct and indirect cost, 88
Documentation and decision tracking, 100
Domain-driven design (DDD), 85
Don'ts of Enterprise Architect
   coerce decisions, 74–75
   evade responsibility, 75–76
   lone wolves, 76–77
   premature compromise, 70–71
   Return on Investment (ROI) ignoring, 71–73
   self-important, self-proclaimed demigods, 76
   slacker, 77
   treating clients dismissively, 73–74
   work in vacuum, 71

E

Efficiency, 143
Elasticity metric, 25
Enterprise Architectural elements
   application architecture, 35–36
   business architecture (BA), 33–34, **34**
   data architecture, 34–35
   infrastructure architecture, 36
   organizational governance, 33
   security architecture, 37
   simplified framework, 32, *33*
Enterprise Architecture, definition, 31
Enterprise architecture objectives
   adaptability, 160
   complexity reduction, 158–159
   cost reduction, 159
   planning support, 161
   standardization, 159–160

Enterprise data model, 44
Errors of commission, 202–203
Errors of omission, 202–203
Event-driven design, 85
Expert, definition, 53
Extensibility metric, 25–26

F

Faulty designs, 22
Fiduciary responsibility, 174–175
50/50 rule, 147
Flawed technology selection, 223–225
Foundational domains, 134
Full lifecycle support, 238

G

Gall's law, 110
Group think, 134

H

Haphazard triage, 197–198
Hardware architecture, 10
Hardware platforms, 59
Homegrown applications, 31
Horizontal scaling, 25

I

Informational triage, 61
Infrastructure architecture, 36
Infrastructure as a Service (IaaS), 237
Infrastructure rules, 237
In-house projects, 123
Integration efforts, 93
Inter-component message protocol, 16
IT architectural models
   controller, 11–12
   data, 12
   view, 11
IT architecture, definition, 10
IT consulting, 136

J

Just-in-Time (JIT) development practices,
  90–92

K

KISS principle, 110

L

Large-scale systems
  augmented projects, 123
  bug hunting, 152
  business functionality, 154
  destination, 148
  development resources, 149
  development team, 154
  documentation rules, 155
  Enterprise Architect (EA) best
    practices, 140–144
  fixed-price projects, 123, 124
  ilities, 155–156
  in-house projects, 123
  initial project estimation, 125
  instrumentation rules, 152
  long-term issues, 151
  micro-mismanagement, 129
  outside consultants, 124
  preliminary requirements, 125
  price architecture, 127–129
  price leadership, 133–135
  price process, 129–133
  problems with teams, 144–148
  project formulation, 124–127
  project governance, 124
  project structure, 123
  public design, 151
  quality, 153
  Rube Goldberg model, 151
  software engineering principles, 151
  software releases, 150
  target topology, 152
  testing rules, 154
  T&M approach, 123
  users rule, 155
  weighing cost *vs.* risk, 128

  working with stakeholders, 135–140
"Latest and greatest" technologies, 30
Leadership, 61, 69, 135, 142, 146, 232
Licensing fees, 92–93
Licensing limitations, 93

M

Machiavellian politics, 196–197
Mentoring, 61–62
Middle-tier design decisions, 83
Monolithic architecture, 14–15, *15*
Multi-tier architecture, *see* N-Tier
    architecture
Municipal planning board
  historic preservation, 29
  Municipal Building Codes, 28
  responsibilities, 28
  Town Vision, 28
  Zoning Board, 29
  Zoning Plan, 28
My Life and Work (Ford), 199
The Mythical Man-Month (Brooks), 215

N

Network Effect, 216, 217
Networking solutions, 59
Next-generation system, 14
NIH syndrome, 202
N-Tier architecture, *16*, 16–17, *17*

O

Occam's Razor Rules, 44, 110–111, 158
One-off technology, 30
Order management systems, 40, 141
Organizational governance, 33
Organization's long-term needs, 13

P

Performance metric, 26
Personal responsibility, 142
Peter principle, 78, 109
Portfolio manager, 133, 170

Post-deployment responsibilities, 238
Price architecture, 127–129
Problem analysis, 173–174
Professional-caliber architecture, 194, 199
Professional Enterprise Architect, 55
Program manager, 133, 170, 228
Programming languages, 60
Project estimating techniques, 125
Project failure
    betting on wrong company, 226
    categories, 191
    conflicting priorities, 207
    deadlines, 194–196
    deficient design, 193–194
    definition, 190
    dismal team composition, 214–221
    errors of omission *vs.* errors of
        commission, 202–203
    "fire and forget" rule, 212
    flawed technology selection, 223–225
    forgetting user community, 207–208
    haphazard design, 209–210
    haphazard triage, 197–198
    ilities, 213
    initial "handwave" estimates, 195
    lackluster applications, 200
    lack of professionalism, 213
    Machiavellian politics, 196–197
    misaligned enterprise architecture,
        211–212
    mitigation techniques, 213
    NIH syndrome, 202
    poor business decisions, 200
    poorly architected projects, 194
    poor project management, 227–232
    professional-caliber architecture, 194
    quixotic scoping, 192–193
    schedule slip, 195
    scope creep, 205–207
    service level agreement (SLA), 213
    technology shortcomings, 222–226
    usage of new product/new version of
        existing product, 225–226
    user indifference, 198–200
    vague user stories, 204–205
    white noise, 210
Project lead, 134

Project management
    Business Analysts (BAs), 229–230
    conflicting objectives, 228–229
    control issues, 227
    ego, 230
    expectations controlling, 231
    fuzzy roles, 227–228
    objectivity lacking, 232
Project manager, 60, 91, 115, 134, 196,
        215–217, 221, 222, 227, 229, 231
Project scoping, 195, 196
Project teams
    civility, 146
    decision avoidance, 145
    degree of dysfunction, 144
    dysfunctional teams, 147
    50/50 rule, 147
    inadequate governance, 145
    leadership, 145
    peer accountability, 146

Q

Quality attributes, 22
Quality of design
    examples, 96
    execution scenarios, 99
    functional requirements, 97
    God Objects, 99
    ilities, 97
    reusability, 98
    solid design, 98
    unwieldy components, 98
Quick and dirty designs, 13, 14
Quixotic scoping, 192–193

R

Refactoring, 88
Reliability metric, 23–24
Required duties, 5
Requirements creep, *see* Scope creep
Restrictive budgets, 14
Resume factor, 116
Return-on-Investment (ROI) analysis, 13,
        41, 72–73
Review cycle, 124

Ripple effects, 84–85
Roles and responsibilities, 158
  advocating, 69–70
  application profusion, 49
  areas of expertise, 58–60
  back channel, 68
  backlog and technical debt, 180
  be responsive, 177
  bugs fixing, 181, 185
  business developments, 184
  business goals, 49
  business strategy, 50
  common sense, 56
  conduct due diligence, 65–66
  conviction, confidence and self-
      assurance, 186
  cozy solutions, 68
  credibility, 186
  culpability, 51
  culture of modern workforce, 235
  data organization, 50
  design change, 53–54
  design feedback, 66
  don'ts of Enterprise Architect, 70–77
  employment evolution, 235
  estimation algorithm, 178
  facilitator, 68
  fiduciary, 68–69
  fundamental project attributes, 180
  homework, 183
  ignorance, 55
  informed decision, 54
  infrastructure components, 49
  integration plans, 235
  leadership, 69
  listening, 67
  lose–lose proposition, 178
  misconceptions, 77–79
  mistakes, 179
  open-door approach, 67
  perfection, 183
  politics rule, 181
  practical realities of life, 184
  professional Enterprise Architect, 55
  project catalyst, 65
  project sponsors, 182
  ripple effects, 177

  risk management, 234
  scheduling, 177, 178
  security issues, 184
  self-confidence, 54
  self-effacing, 181
  significant decisions, 179
  skillsets, 60–64
  stepwise refinement, 184
  strategy development, 56–58
  support test teams, 185
  system testing, 52
  unwieldy applications, 49
  validate, review, and spot-check, 182
  vetting process, 66
  workforce trends, 184
Rube Goldberg model, 151
Rule of Three, 75, 140

S

Sales technique, 138
Scalability metric, 24–25
Scope creep
  causes of, 205
  consequences of, 206
  definition, 205
  safeguards, 206
Security architecture, 11, 37
Security measures, 96
Security rules, 239
Security technologies, 59
Self-proclaimed Enterprise Architect, 55
Service level agreement (SLA), 213
Service-oriented architecture (SOA),
      17–18, *18*
Skillsets
  accountability, 64
  advocate, 62
  attributes, 162
  "back channel" information, 166
  champion, 164
  commitment, 61
  communication, 62
  confessor, 62–63, 165–166
  informational triage, 61
  information sharing, 162
  leadership, 61

mentoring, 61–62
moralist, 166–167
negotiator, 168–169
objectivity rules, 167
pedagogue, 163
politician, 63–64
pragmatist, 165
project management, 60
realist, 167–168
reluctant advocate, 164–165
router, 162–163
strategist, 167
visionary, 163–164
Socratic method, 138
Soft landing, 190
Software design
architecture *vs.* design, *103*,
103–105, *104*
compromise cost, 107
definition, 102
inflexibility cost, 108
objective of, 105–107
Software Development Lifecycle
(SDLC), 59
Software methodology
comprehension, 129–130
construction, 130
evolution, 130
foolproof techniques, 130
knee-jerk reactions, 132
project success, 131
schedules, 132–133
shortcuts, 132
talent, 131
verification, 130
Solutions architecture, 11
Strategy development, 56–58
System design issues
Candy factor, 116–117
degree of professionalism, 117
evaluation criteria, 118
feedback loop, 118
flagrant assumptions, 111–113
impatience, 114
instrumentation and testability, 114
intransigence, 113

lack of traceability, 114–115
level of respective incompetence, 109
now-retired legacy system, 119
Occam's Razor, 110–111
Peter principle, 109
procrastination, 113
shortcuts, 115
simplification, 118
stepwise refinement, 109–110
technical depth, 116
System performance, 43
Systems architecture, 11

T

Talent, 101, 131, 144, 221, 227
team composition
adding new members to
team, 216
collaboration, 217–219
deadwood, 220
esprit de corps, 215
interpersonal skills, 219–220
lack of talent, 221
management overhead, 216–217
Network Effect, 216, 217
reasonable schedules, 215
staff size increasing, 215–216
team-building moments, 215
Technical Debt, 87–89
Technological vision, 56, 57
Testability metric, 27
Transition plan, 57
Two-tier design, 85

U

User indifference, 198–200
User interface design and technology, 83

V

Value proposition, 37–40, 237
Vendor support, 93
Vendor viability, 93
Vertical scaling, 25

W

Web-based retail application, 17
Workday of Enterprise Architects
    assisting project team members, 169
    common duties, 172–173
    common tasks, 173

    job requirement, 171
    meeting agendas, 170
    meeting preparation, 170
    own responsibilities, 169
    primary responsibilities, 171
wrapper functions, 94

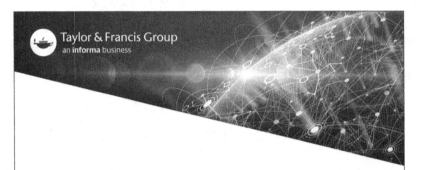

Printed in the United States
by Baker & Taylor Publisher Services